Contents

Introduction

From old 'wives' tales to modern science, horse whorls have always been a matter of interest. People have noticed unique and unusual characteristics in their animals and made note of them when they come across them again. They began to notice similarities between animals who shared them. Over time, these observations evolved into folklore.

Until science caught up and people were able to explain the why behind the superstitions.

When the fetus is developing in the womb, before the eighteenth week of gestation, the skin and the brain develop simultaneously. There are different theories as to exactly how that growth affects the hair.

One theory is that the growth tendencies of the hair follicles in whorls are influenced by the pressure of the growing brain on the scalp. Cranio-cerebral anomalies can change the hair-patterns.

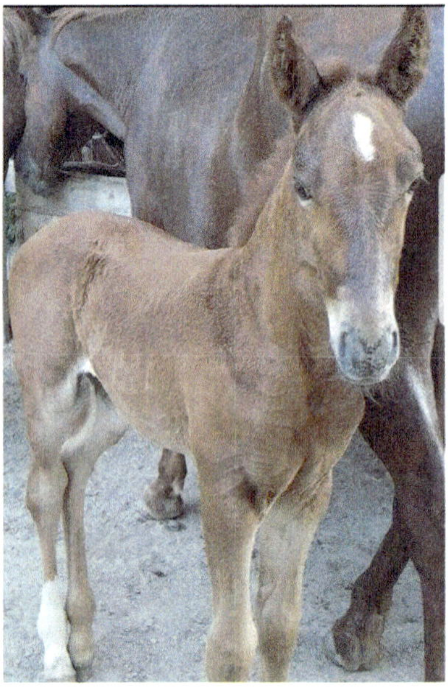

We can see wide set ears, a broad forehead, and an interesting whorl on this foal. He should be a very smart, sensitive, curious adult.

3rd Edition

Understanding Horse Whorls

Another theory is that higher or lower metabolic activity in certain areas could result in more active growth, leading to uneven development on one side of the follicle compared to the other.

Whatever the exact cause, when extra activity is taking place in one certain area, it leaves a mark in the skin above that area, forming a whorl. The same is true of the entire body and whorls can show up anywhere, letting us have a special peek into the inner workings of the horse.

All animals with hair have whorls, and there have been many more studies done on people than horses. We can assume that the meanings and causes found in studies done on people will apply to horses in many, if not all, findings. This allows us to access a much greater amount of information on the subject.

All things with hair have whorls including goats. Here there are two marking the spot where horns will emerge, plus another whorl in the middle.

The Hairy Ball Theorem

Named in all seriousness, I'm sure, this theorem is lucky to have such a catchy name because reading it is enough to make anyone's eyes cross. In short, it means that you could not comb the hair on a hairy ball flat without it leaving a whorl somewhere.

The actual Hairy Ball Theorem reads:

"The **hairy ball theorem** of algebraic topology (sometimes called the **hedgehog theorem** in Europe) states that there is no nonvanishing continuous tangent vector field on even-dimensional n-spheres. For the ordinary sphere, or 2-sphere, if *f* is a continuous function that assigns a vector in $\mathbf{R}^3$ to every point *p* on a sphere such that *f*(*p*) is always tangent to the sphere at *p*, then there is at least one *p* such that *f*(*p*) = 0."

A continuous tangent vector field on a 2-sphere with only one pole, in this case a dipole field.

See? I told you it would make your eyes cross.

Because everything with hair has whorls, there are theories and superstitions surrounding the whorls on every type of animal, including humans. Some of these theories are well studied and documented, others not so much.

Looking at horse's whorls is still more art than science. Although we know there are meanings associated with all whorls, we still don't know exactly what those meanings are.

The ones we do know are subject to different interpretations. Many will say double whorls are a bad sign, and any number higher than that is supposed to be "complicated". There is still no word as to what complicated might mean.

That is before we even begin to get into markings such as Allah's thumbprint, a sign of good luck, or the shredded collar, a long whorl down the front of the neck said to bring bad luck. There is a physical manifestation that the markings are a symptom of, but they are not good or bad luck.

Separating superstition from science gets to be tricky.

Superstitions

The superstitions that come with horse whorls can be fun to hear. Even if they are a bit far-fetched at times. They may not appear fact-based, but that doesn't make them any less enjoyable to read about.

I have heard it said that whorls are battle scars from a past life. Those scars go on to influence the way a horse moves and acts in this life. That one is the most fanciful of them all.

Indonesia has a rich and fascinating horse culture with many myths surrounding horse whorls. Horses with high double whorls are called "kembang sepasang," or flower pair, and are said to be good for your love life.

Whorls in the center of the chest are called “paku dada,” chest nail, and the horses who possess them are believed to be stubborn and lacking in intelligence, At the same time they are thought to be great competition horses who are likely to win! An interesting combination.

Whorls below eye level are called "turun tangis," which translates to “cry.” These horses are supposed to be trouble causers. That has a ring of truth to it. If well managed, they are said to be smart and good performance horses. That one does sound like a good description of a horse with a low whorl!

I wonder if this whorl is low enough to count as Turun Tangis?

If a horse has whorls on the chest, one on the right and two on the left, it is called "Bahurekso." This whorl pattern is supposed to bring its rider safety when used in battle. If we look at the whorl pattern, it is possible that there is a cause for this superstition. An extra whorl on the left side would cause a horse to turn that way more easily. Assuming this superstition was referring to fighting with swords or some other weapon in hand, most people are right-handed. A horse turning easily away from your weapon hand could make it easier to wield it in battle.

Throughout history, horses have been very important as a tool of war, so it isn't surprising that many myths surrounding whorls involve their abilities in battle.

The whorl of the spur is when the flank whorl tips upward. This whorl is said to mean safety in battle and was carried by the Byerley Turk. On the other hand, if the flank whorl curves downward it is a sign of prosperity. I can only imagine what is meant by upwards? Downwards? All the flank whorls I have seen go up and down!

A whorl on the fetlock comes with a very colorful story. Known as the whorl of theft, the horse who bares it is said to spend night and day praying, "Oh, my God! Grant that I may be stolen or my master die." Not a particularly pleasant myth.

Would this flank whorl count as being curved upwards?

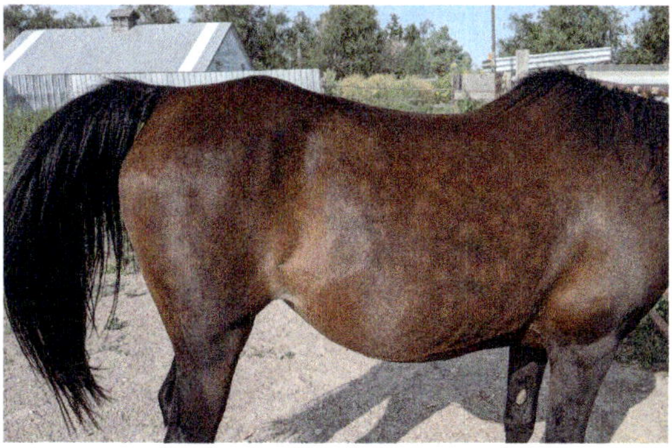

Nature vs Nurture

As with everything in life, the roles of nature versus nurture play a large role in what behaviors a horse will display. A horse with a high whorl who has been raised with a lot of support and encouragement to be brave and curious will not show the same behavior as a high whorled horse who has been treated harshly.

The same applies to whorls on the body. A horse with a large flared neck whorl, who is ridden without learning to use his body and give to bit pressure, will not ride well. They will end up with a terrible ewe neck, nose in the air, hollow back, unable to work or move efficiently. When taught to be round and soft, the same horse will be much healthier and more comfortable. He may never become an upper-level dressage horse, but he can still be a good riding horse.

Just because a horse doesn't show the expected qualities of the whorls they carry doesn't mean they aren't affected by them. There are exceptions to every rule, and the life an animal leads can change the way they handle their natural-born traits.

How we nurture horses with different whorl types makes a big difference. A high whorl set to our right makes an emotional, sensitive, and responsive horse. It's a delightful whorl to have, when the horse is worked with using kind understanding training methods.
The same horse can be terrified of everything and reactive to the extreme if trained harshly.

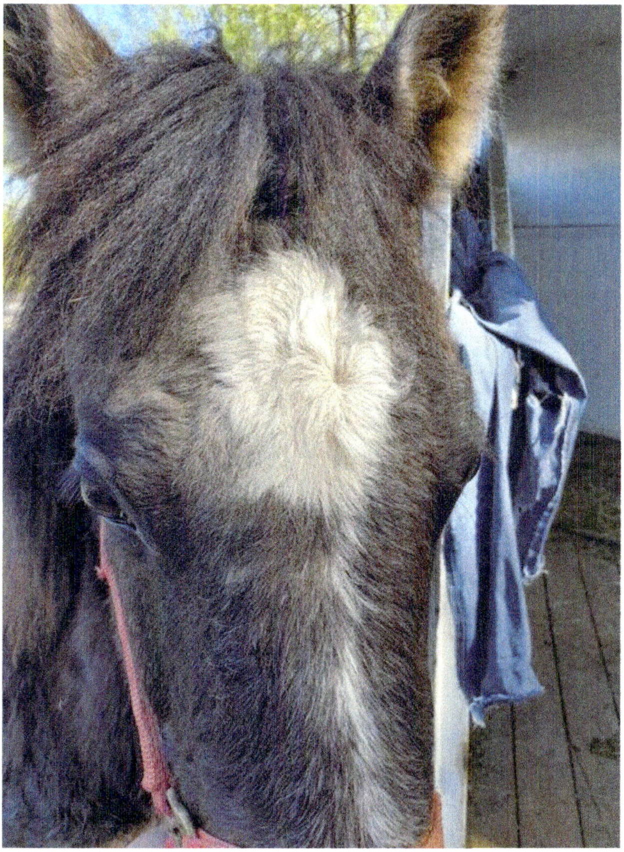

There's No Right, Wrong, Good Or Bad Whorl

A horse with any whorl can work out great with one person and be a terrible match for another. There are also differences in the extremes to which characteristics will be shown, with some horses displaying great extremes while others barely show a trait.

The reading of whorls is meant as a loose guide to help us find the training and handling methods that best suit our horses.

Whorls are **not** set in stone proof of character.

Here we can see a horse with a beautifully stacked double whorl. They are intelligent and energetic, making them a lot of fun for experienced riders. However, they are not well suited to timid beginners.

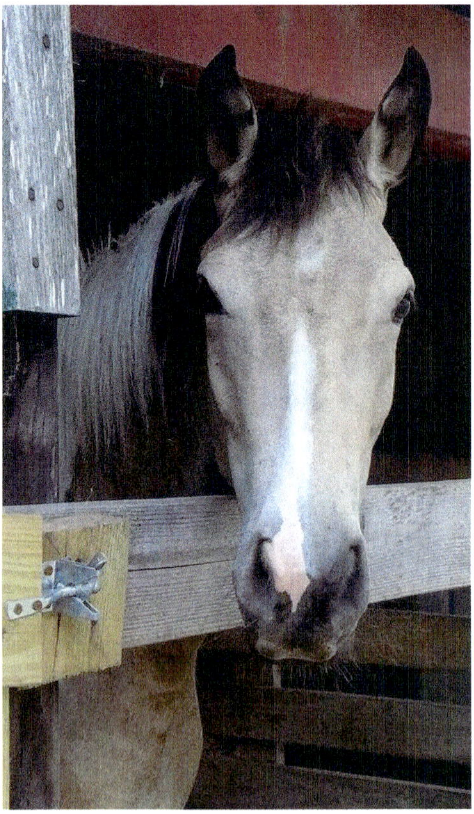

Whorls Are Outward Indicators Of What Is Happening Inside

It is often said that different whorl patterns or head shapes are the cause of certain behaviors in horses. In reality, they are just an outward indication of the underlying cause and not necessarily the cause itself.

A whorl can be created if a muscle didn't develop completely or if it is over-developed. The whorl is just an exterior mark. We can make use of these marks to get insight to the horse's character that maybe we wouldn't discover without lots of time and effort.

If a horse has a Roman nose, it may mean he is tough or perhaps stubborn, but it didn't cause the personality traits. Genetics are a fascinating and complicated thing. If we breed for one trait it can lead to the presence of other seemingly unrelated traits without our realization.

A mare and foal with matching whorls. Their heads are the same, down to the way their noses are quirked to the side.

As we breed for one trait, say, when creating a breed, genetic variants will occur within that group. New mutations emerge, many of which have no functional consequence, and by random chance, spread within the breed's population. These genetic shifts within a breed, or breeding population, occur independently of similar random shifts occurring in the rest of the horse world.

For example, say we are breeding for a horse that is dependable. A very straight profile on a nearly perfectly rectangular head may not be something we have any interest in. As we breed more hard-working horses we can trust, more of them end up with the same head type. This head type was not created on purpose, but it has become a trait that is now associated with a dependable temperament.

The opposite can also be true. Maybe we aren't paying attention to temperament. Perhaps we are breeding for the head type. If an extreme dish is stylish and what we are looking for, we can unintentionally create a hot, reactive temperament in the breed without meaning to.

A high center whorl, cheek whorls, and large whorls in the throatlatch area tell us a lot about this foal. All of these are things that were likely not bred for on purpose.

It should be no surprise that a study that looked at over four thousand thoroughbreds in Japan found that fifty-five percent of them had high whorls. Why wouldn't a horse that is bred to run have whorls that show a horse who wants to move?

That same study also found that the position of horse whorls was more likely to be passed on from parents to offspring than the number of whorls. Often a parent with multiple whorls will produce a good percentage of offspring with the same number of whorls they have. One particular double whorled stud had a record of producing fifty percent double whorled foals. However, we don't know what whorls the dams of the foals carried.

There is no reason to think that we haven't been accidentally breeding these 'tells' into horses since time immemorial. Why wouldn't a physical trait be passed along with a temperament type?

Draft horse heads typically show tough, steady, dependable horses. Useful in a draft horse, but the head type wasn't bred for on purpose.

This image shows an almost perfectly rectangular profile that suggests a calm, steady horse. This is a common trait, bred on accident into old working breeds that had to be quiet enough for the family to handle, but have enough go to work a field all day or trot to town.

Whorls Don't Change With Age

The whorls a horse is born with are the whorls a horse will have for life.

Because whorls don't change with age, they are often used by breed associations for identification purposes. They can also be used to get an idea of what a foal will be like when they mature.

Many features of the head will stay the same as horses age; a dished nose or broad forehead won't go away. In contrast, other features, such as brain muscle and complicated chins, can mature and amplify over the years.

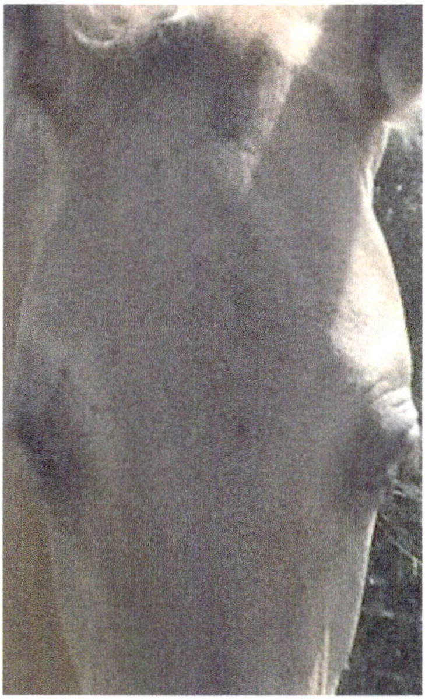

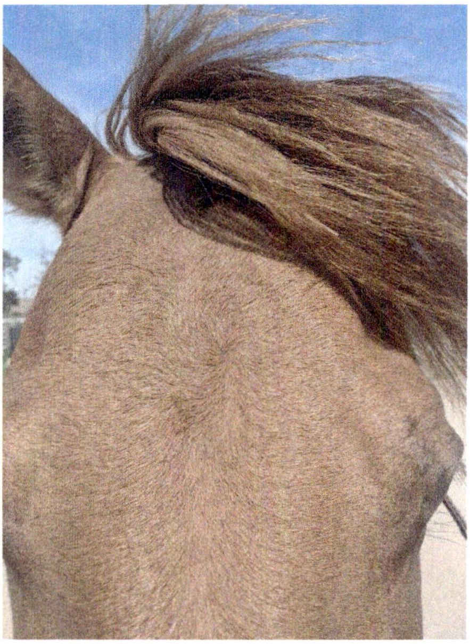

The broad forehead, widely spaced ears, and barely-there second whorl haven't changed from weanling to adult.

Some Things Will Change Though

While whorls won't change or move with age, some aspects of a horse's features can.

A horse's features can change if they go from a happy environment with good training conditions to a bad one or vice versa. Such changes can cause eyes to go from open and soft to hard and deep with wrinkles around them.

Chins can relax and soften when a horse loses fear and stress. Mouths can lose tension. Even the profile can seem to change as features relax or open up. Winter coats can hide or exaggerate whorls, changing appearances completely with the passing of seasons. The whorls are still the same under the coat, they are just hidden temporarily.

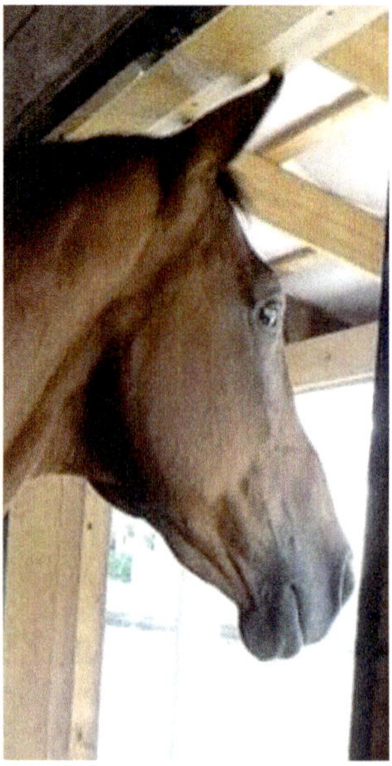

In the before picture, on the left, we see eyes tight and withdrawn, nostrils small, profile round. In a later picture, after settling health issues and retraining, his eyes are bright, nostrils open. He looks far more interested and alert, happier with life in general.

Types Of Whorls

Whorls come in all different shapes and sizes. There are a few that are more common though. These whorls can be found anywhere on a horse's body. Their different shapes all mean something, so it is important to be familiar with them.

Whorl:

A simple, common, basic whorl. The hair grows in a tight circle, clockwise or counterclockwise. A horse will tend to bend around these whorls if they are on the body, especially if they are on one side and not the other.

Feather:

A long line in the hair with the hair growing away from the center line, resembling a feather. On the forehead, a straight line of feathering often means the horse is left-brained.

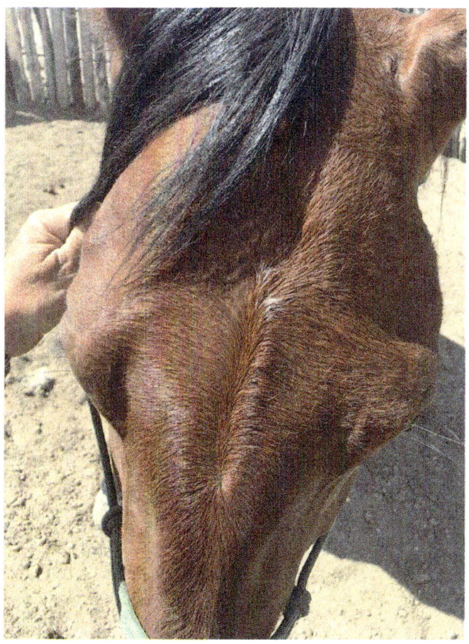

Open Splaying:

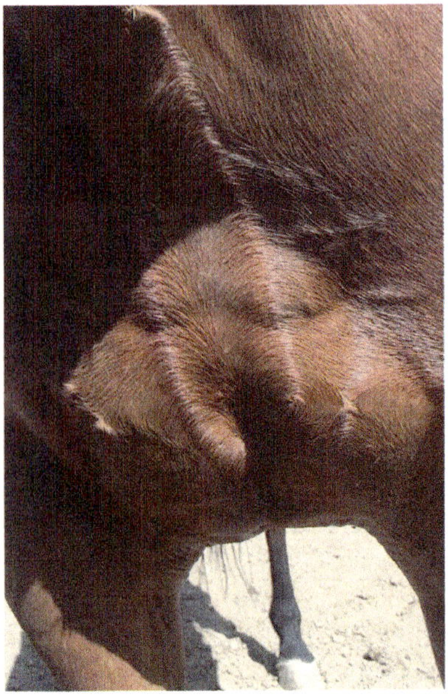

Different than a feathered whorl. Instead of a centerline, the open splaying whorls are smooth through the middle. Large and sometimes long, open splaying whorls usually have a distinct outer ring of hair forming an outline. They can also be a patch of hair growing differently than the surrounding hair, without the distinct outer ring. On the body, a horse will tend to push into this type of whorl.

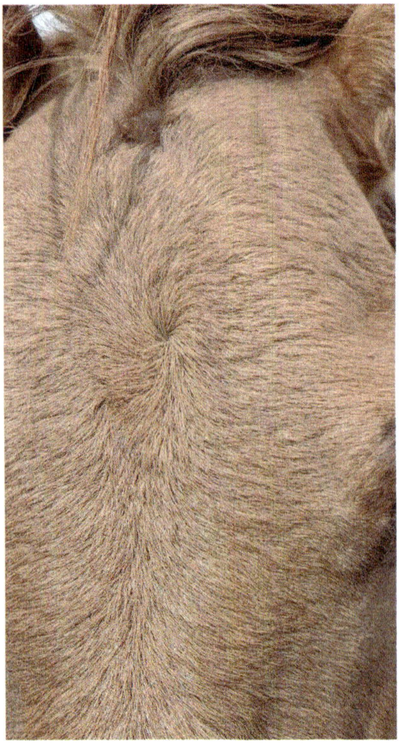

Ghost:

A faint hint of where a whorl might be. Sometimes they look like a place where the hair has been brushed wrong and might be standing up a little. These ghost whorls should still be counted as a whorl. They affect behavior almost as strongly as if the whorl had fully formed.

This horse has a double whorl.

Zipper Whorl:

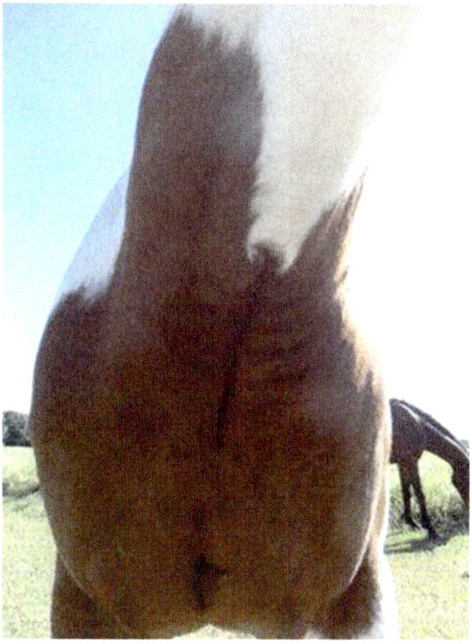

A line where the hair grows towards itself from both directions. Long and narrow, the hair meets in a raised ridge down the middle.

These have the opposite effect of the open splaying whorl. Instead of creating a downward pulling effect on the horse's muscling, they cause the horse to lift up, away from the whorl.

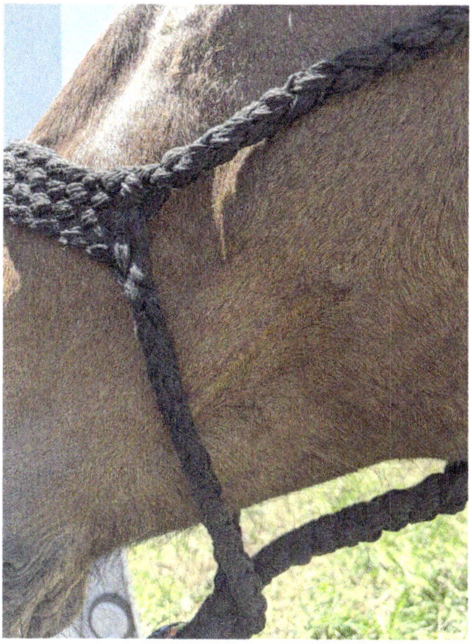

Line Or Wheat Whorl:

Like the zipper whorl, but without the line of raised hair down the middle. This marking is a simple line in the hair, not a round whorl, and not open splaying.

The hair will be raised in one direction and overlap the hair that lays flat, but there isn't hair coming from the other direction to meet it like a zipper whorl.

The Brain

The brain is very specialized in the jobs carried out by the individual and separate halves. The makeup of the brain itself is even different in each half. The left hemisphere of the brain is made of more gray matter. This cerebral material is a thin and tough surface, also known as the cortex. The right brain consists of more white matter. This is the supporting tissue underneath grey matter with longer axons that connect to modules farther away from the white matter. This distance allows the development of broader, more open concepts than the tightly packed neurons of the left brain's gray matter, which processes close details and facts.

When describing a horse's temperament and personality, one way to simplify the explanations is to refer to the part of the brain the horse tends to operate from.

There are four different behavior types, not four quarters, but four overlapping halves. Introvert and extrovert, and right-brain and left-brain.

This explanation is a great oversimplification because the two halves of the brain work together. No animal only functions naturally in one hemisphere or the other. A horse can show more characteristics of the functions that one side of the brain offers, and that is what we would call their dominant brain type.

All horses have some traits of each brain type. Some have far more of one type than another, while others are evenly balanced. When we say extreme right-brain, it means that they show a lot of right-brain tendencies. This does not mean they won't show any left-brain tendencies.

A horse can be equally right and left-brain, resulting in nicely balanced traits or switching back and forth depending on the circumstances.

We hope that a perfectly centered whorl will show a horse who draws equally from all four quadrants of the brain.

Right Brain

The right side of the human brain controls emotion.

The right side of our brain controls the left side of our body, which includes the left side of our face. Most people are far more expressive on the left side of their face. If one eyebrow can be raised it is usually the left one, if a lip is sneered it is typically to the left. Looking at other people and trying to judge their feelings or emotions we tend to look at the left side of their faces and when confronted with something frightening people focus on it with the left eye.

This is important when we move the discussion to horses because a scared horse will often spook and leap to a position where the left side of their body faces whatever scared them. That is the right side of the brain kicking in, processing what happened and determining if they should be frightened.

A typical right brain whorl, high and set slightly to our right when facing the horse

We assume that horses put us on their left side because it is where we traditionally handle them. However, unhandled mustangs, straight off the range, will naturally try to keep us on their left sides too. This behavior is not a result of them being taught that this is how it should be. Instead, this is a natural reaction that puts people in view of the eye that communicates directly with the right side of their brain, allowing them to process fear and react appropriately.

Horses are capable of recognizing human expression. They can tell if someone is happy or mad and remember this the next time they see that person. This ability is a result of the right brain at work.

A horse's right brain processes their emotions. When the right brain is in control the horse is a subject of their emotions and, as a result, their feelings. They want to be loved, they want to be appreciated, they want to sit in our lap and be hugged.

The brain's right side is all about the senses. What the horse feels and sees takes priority over thinking when it comes to this side of the brain. Unfortunately, that also means a horse operating from their right brain can be fearful and reactive to stimuli.

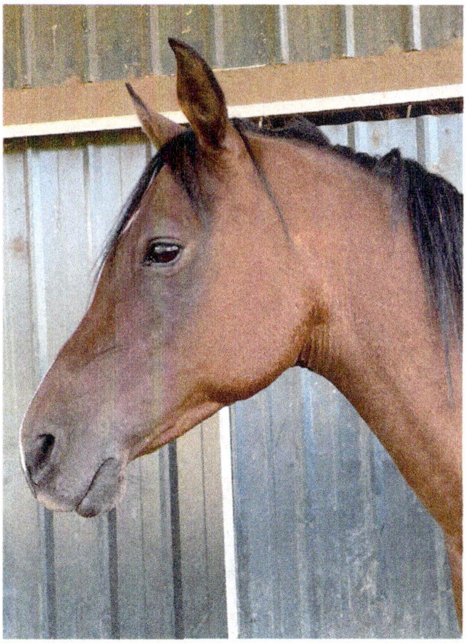

A hard round eye and dished profile, show a right brain horse.

Right brain horses don't miss anything that is going on around them. This alert and aware behavior can result in nervousness. Their nervousness can be soothed by repetition and predictability.

Left Brain

The left side of the brain in humans controls language, logic, and facts. It is all about thinking things through carefully and thoroughly before acting. Horses may not have a verbal language, but they are capable of logic; cold, calm, logic.

Left-brain horses are the ones who will undo gate latches, they will untie themselves, they will untie other horses! A left-brain horse wants a game, a challenge, something to keep their busy minds occupied.

A left-brain horse can be one who fears nothing. They can also be the one who sees no reason to listen. When they are interested and want something, a left-brain horse will demand you give it to them.

My left-brain extrovert horse will stand out in the pasture and demand that I come work with him. He will call, scream, and bang on the gate. He's all about me, me, me!

They need work with you to be interesting in order to keep their attention. Once they are bored they see no reason to pay attention to you. Work time needs to be fast-paced and interesting. Boredom and repetition are the greatest enemy of a left-brain horse.

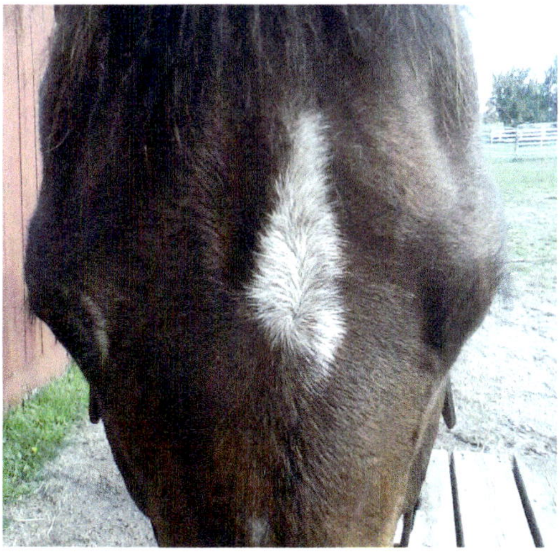

The feathering coming from the whorl that is common to left brain horses.

Extrovert

Like in people, an extroverted horse is a social creature. An extrovert likes to visit others and see what is going on in life. They want to be there for the excitement and they may create their own excitement if they get bored. When an extrovert isn't being kept entertained they will go looking for ways to entertain themselves. They usually have a great sense of humor and will spook, take things apart, gallop around their pasture, or let themselves out of the pasture.

Extroverts are very invested in the external world and everything going on around them. They want to be on the move all of the time.

They are the hot horses who want to be in the front. Extroverts can get carried away with their desire to be moving and need help to calm down before they can pay attention.

A high whorl and pricked ears are common to extroverts.

Introvert

An introverted horse is content within themselves. They are busy thinking and processing the information around them. Sometimes people make the mistake of underestimating their intelligence because they don't respond immediately, which is a major mistake. Introverts can be extremely intelligent, they just don't run around telling everyone about it like an extrovert does. They have a quiet, droll sense of humor.

Introverts like their space. They can be overwhelmed by too much excitement around them. This can cause them to withdraw even further and not respond to overwhelming attempts to get their attention or make them listen.

Instead of trying to make an introvert do anything, they need to be given a reason to listen. Explain to them WHY you want them to do something and make it worth their while. They don't want to move in the first place. Introverts strongly dislike lots of movement without any apparent purpose.

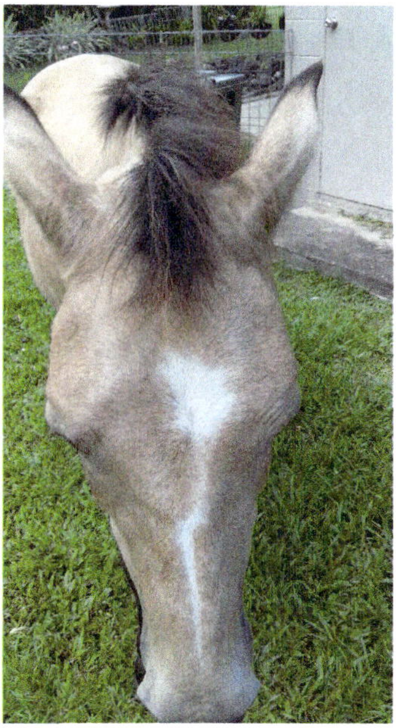

Low whorl and ears carried back are typical features of an introvert.

Horse Personality Guide

There are still many whorls we don't know the meaning of. Using the Horse Personality Guide can be an effective way of finding similarities between unknown whorl types.

With one method of comparison, similarities in brain types can be determined through the identification of matching whorls. The owners of horses with three whorls all mark them as falling into the left brain extrovert category, for example. This is easier than going by vague comparisons that can mean different things to different people.

It can also be fun to compare our horses' whorls to what we know. This chart can help you find your horse's dominant brain quadrants.

Go through and mark your horse according to each question. Find the areas where your horse scores the highest. It is possible for your horse to score evenly through all of the quadrants. That shows a very well rounded horse and is what we would hope to find of a horse with a single center whorl.

Most horses will be higher in one or two areas, introvert or extrovert, right-brain or left-brain. These results shows they are a right-brain extrovert or a left-brain introvert.

INSTRUCTIONS
Enter 1, 2, or 3 in each box according to what best suits your horse.

1 = Disagree
2 = Neutral
3 = Agree

Add up your scores and mark the areas that best describe your horse.

Extrovert

- [ ] Tends to carry his ears pricked forward
- [ ] Has lots of energy and likes to be moving
- [ ] Goes faster if I loosen up the reins
- [ ] Learns things very quickly and will often outsmart me
- [ ] Thinks up ways to amuse himself often getting into trouble
- [ ] Panics if too much pressure is placed on him
- [ ] Tends to run when spooked
- [ ] Is very alert and notices everything that goes on around him
- [ ] Thinks he's a puppy dog and wants to sit on my lap

Left Brain

- [ ] Usually the brave one in a group
- [ ] Loves to explore new things
- [ ] Will sometimes get pushy with me if he wants something
- [ ] Is unconcerned about many things that usually scare horses
- [ ] Will ignore me if I try to make him do something he doesn't want to
- [ ] Will think up ways to play with objects or other horses that often gets him in trouble
- [ ] Likes to be petted enthusiastically and firmly
- [ ] Will fight if too much pressure is placed on him
- [ ] Main love in life is food!

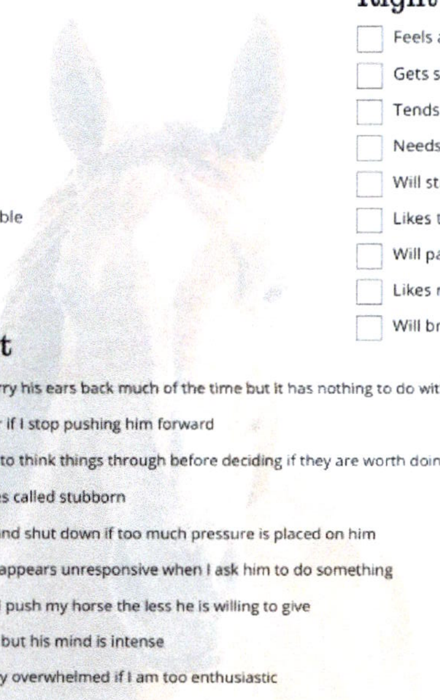

Right Brain

- [ ] Feels all the emotions strongly
- [ ] Gets scared by new or noisy stimulus
- [ ] Tends to carry his head high and on alert
- [ ] Needs me to offer comfort and support when worried
- [ ] Will strike out in defense if pushed too hard
- [ ] Likes to be petted gently and softly or he gets worried
- [ ] Will panic and bolt if too much pressure is placed on him
- [ ] Likes repetition; it calms and comforts him
- [ ] Will break down completely when punished or handled roughly

Introvert

- [ ] Tends to carry his ears back much of the time but it has nothing to do with being upset
- [ ] Goes slower if I stop pushing him forward
- [ ] Needs time to think things through before deciding if they are worth doing
- [ ] Is sometimes called stubborn
- [ ] Will freeze and shut down if too much pressure is placed on him
- [ ] Sometimes appears unresponsive when I ask him to do something
- [ ] The harder I push my horse the less he is willing to give
- [ ] Moves slow but his mind is intense
- [ ] Can be easily overwhelmed if I am too enthusiastic

Facial Whorls

Whorls on a horse's forehead are the most common and basic.

Single Center Whorl

A single center whorl, directly between the eyes, neither higher than eye level nor below eye level, is normal; it doesn't mean very much on its own.

When a horse has this whorl, we need to look at the rest of the head to get an idea of the horse's temperament.

High Single Whorl

A single whorl above eye level, but still in the center, will usually mean the horse is an extrovert who is interested in what is going on around them, curious, with a very active mind. Usually, these horses are energetic and a bit on the hot side.

Sometimes it is only their mind that is always working in overdrive. A horse with a high whorl is smart and sensitive. They often work best with a confident rider who will take the horse's intelligence into account and not ride roughshod over him.

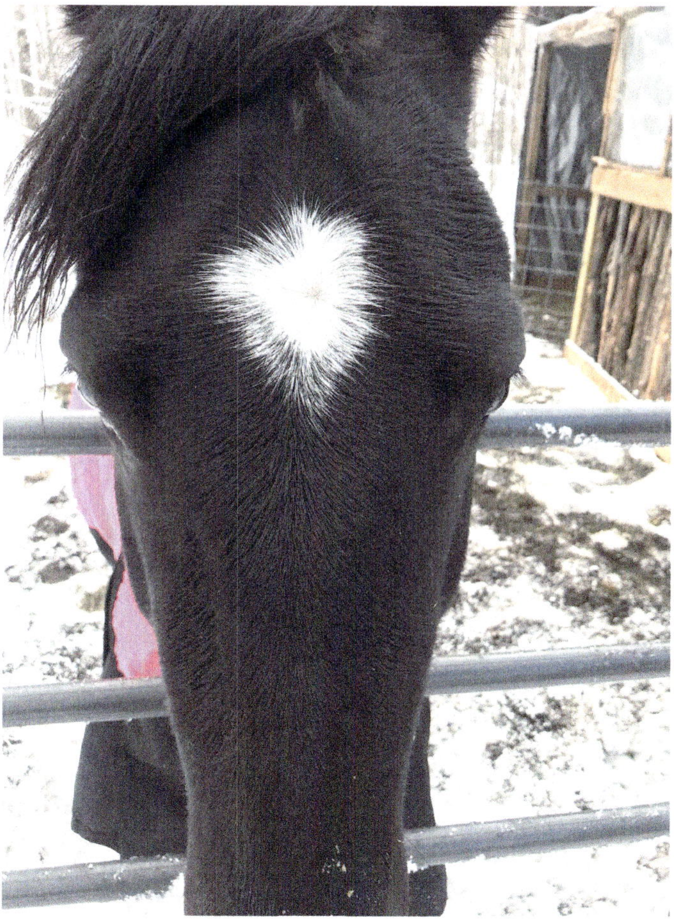

Low Single Whorl

A single low whorl, below eye level, shows an introverted personality.

Most mules have a very low whorl. They are thinkers; quiet, and hesitant to make any rash moves. They want to look at a problem from all angles before making up their minds. Horses with low whorls are very smart but not obvious about showing you what they are planning. A horse with a low whorl needs someone who will be patient with them and give them the time they need without mistaking them for being lazy or stupid.

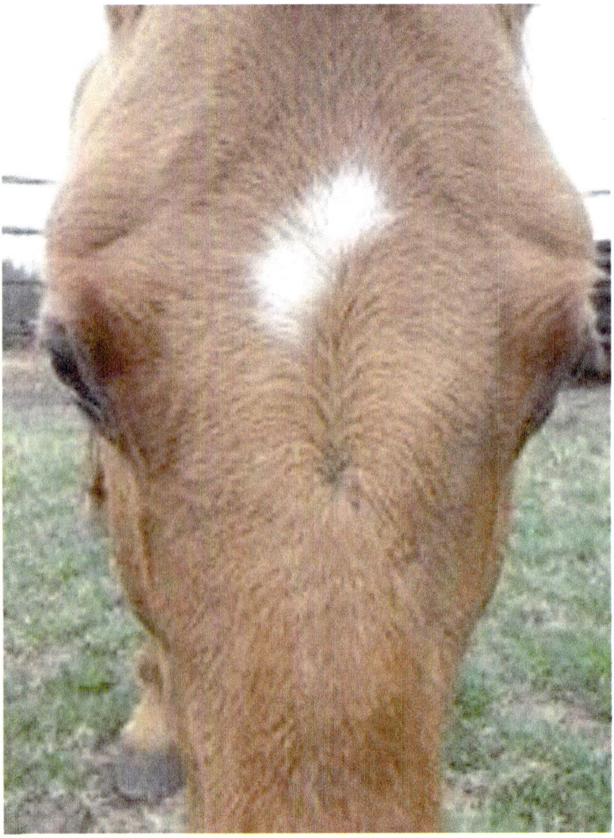

Left Or Right Whorl

When a whorl is placed to the right or left, it shows dominance of one side of the brain. It isn't true that the sides of the brain don't work together. A horse can transfer learning from one side of the body to another, but that doesn't mean there aren't differences in how each side of the brain works.

The theory that we have a dominant brain side has been, if not disproven, found to not be exactly correct. That doesn't mean horses can't have a stronger side, like people who are right or left-handed. When one side of a horse's brain is stronger, it can lead to certain personality traits.

Like a right-handed person is said to be left-brained, a horse with a whorl on the right side of his forehead will be left-brained and vice versa. That means it's easiest to refer to whorls by whether they are on our right or left, as we face the horse, so it matches up with the brain side.

A horse with a whorl to our left will most likely be left-brain, calm, confident, and not worried about things.

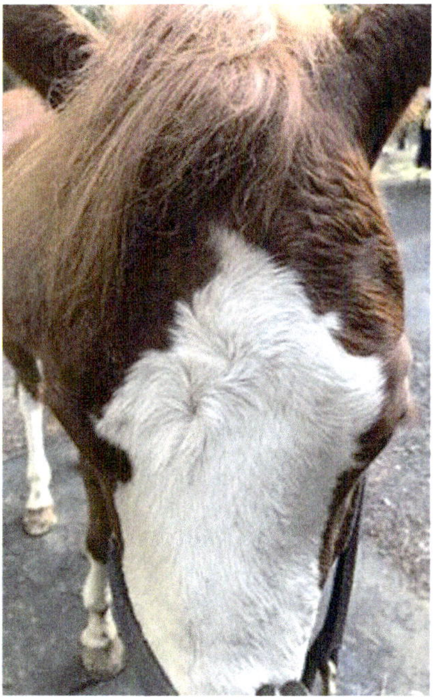

This horse has a whorl placed to our left. He could be introverted or extroverted. The feathering coming from the whorl also shows left-brain tendencies. It is in the shape of an S which is said to mean the horse is accident-prone.

A horse with a whorl to our right will be right-brained, more emotional, less secure, more reactive.

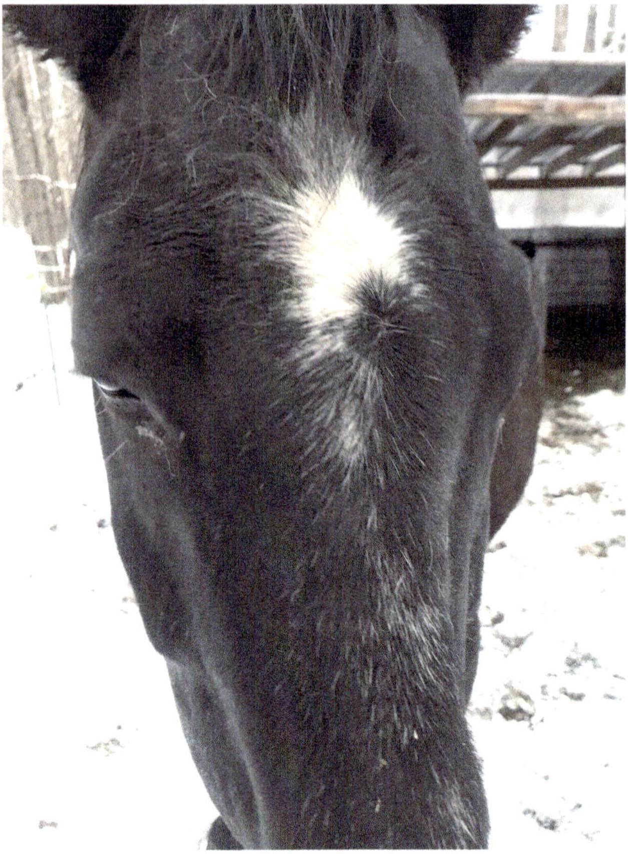

The farther to either side a whorl is, the more pronounced the trait. A whorl that is just slightly off-center will barely show the right or left brain. A whorl nearly off the side of the head will have strongly pronounced traits.

The direction hair swirls inside of a whorl is also supposed to tell us about sidedness. A whorl that has a counter-clockwise swirl is generally left-sided and a clockwise swirl is usually right-sided. In this case sided means a preference for one lead over the other or a tendency to turn a certain direction when they spook.

Feathering

When the hair leaving the whorl is split and leaves a trail, it is called feathering. Feathering is said to show a friendly horse. I have also found it to be a sign of a left brain horse, calm, confident, fond of people.

Sometimes it is barely noticeable, and other times it is the most noticeable thing about a horse. Many low whorls have long, well-defined feathering that clearly shows a left-brain introvert. The definition and length of the feathering doesn't seem to make any difference.

Feathering in the shape of an S is said to show a horse who tends to be accident-prone and who gets hurt regularly.

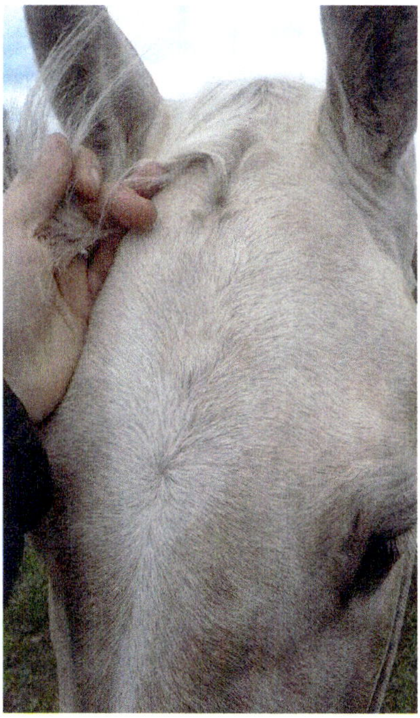

Barely visible feathering

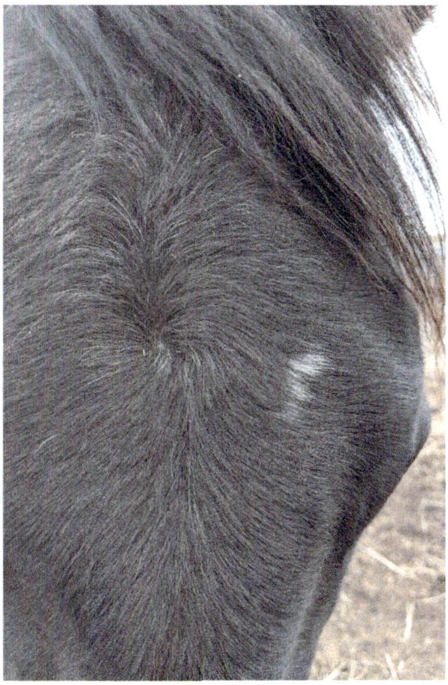

Clearly visible feathering

Line Whorl

When the forehead whorl is a line, instead of a spot where the hair circles, it is called a line whorl. Line whorls show the same temperament type as a feathering coming up from the whorl. Horses with a line are generally left-brained. Left-brain horses are confident, friendly, curious, and willful.

The line itself doesn't tell us if the horse is an introvert or an extrovert. Like any other whorl, where the line is placed can give us clues to that.

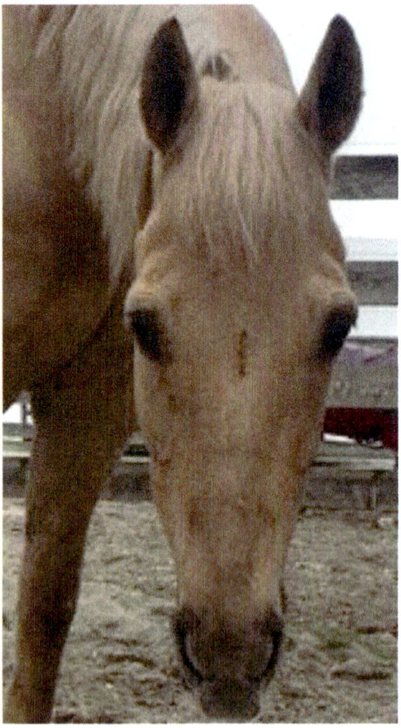

Double Forelock

Occasionally we will see a horse with a large tuft of hair growing out of the middle of their forehead.

This doesn't have any meaning outside of the location of the whorl.

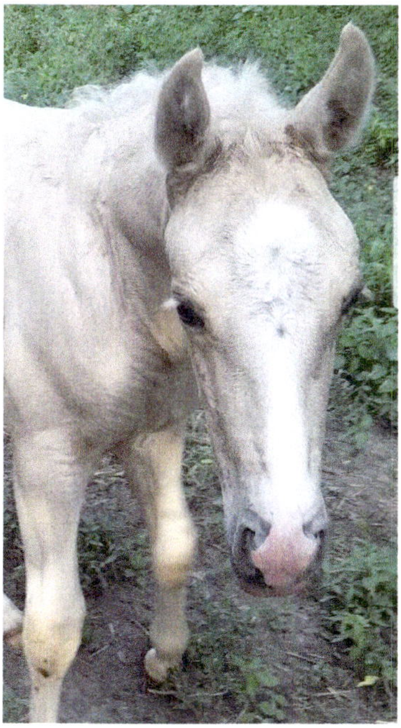

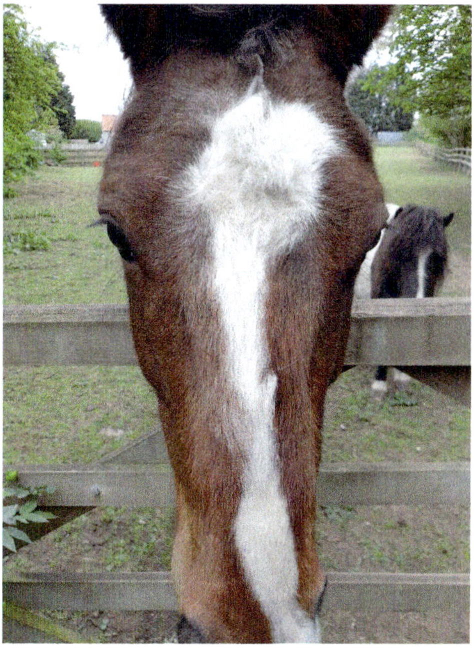

No one knows for sure what the cause is. It is theorized that it could be misplaced hair cells, especially in breeds that are bred for lots of hair and traits such as mustaches.

One trend among mares who have given birth to foals with double forelocks is extreme sickness during pregnancy, from colic to infection. Correlation does not necessarily equal causation, but it is an interesting connection.

No Whorls

Some horses will have no whorl at all! While this is common in cattle and donkeys, it rarely occurs in horses. Without higher numbers of horses to gather information from, we can look across the different species to find the parallels.

An absence of whorls has been connected to animals that have right-brain extrovert temperaments. They are commonly reactive and alert.

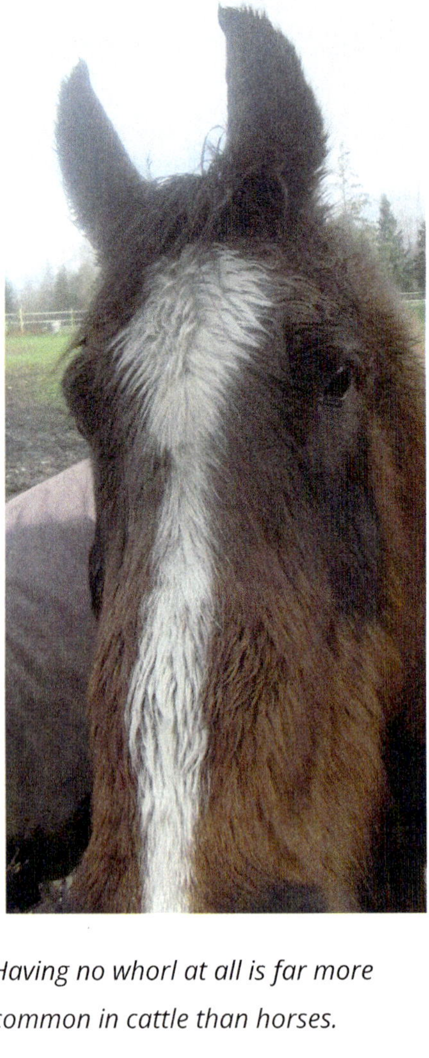

This horse is loved despite, or for, his tendency to 'disapparate'. He seems to disappear from one place and reappear in another for no apparent reason, and usually without the rider.

Having no whorl at all is far more common in cattle than horses.

Cheek Whorls

Once taken as a sign of bad luck that can bring ruin to the owner of a horse with this whorl, cheek whorls are fairly common to horses. Superstitions are normally just that, but sometimes they originate from facts.

Of course these whorls aren't actually bad luck but they can have some interesting effects.

When there is a whorl on one side of the cheek but not the other, just like anywhere on a horse, there will be unevenness. The horse will prefer to turn towards the whorl.

That unevenness can be carried internally too. Often the horse will tend to clinch the TMJ, or temporomandibular joint. This is where the lower jaw or mandible connects with the upper jaw or maxilla, through the temporal bone of the skull.

This is a very important joint. Tightness or inflammation in the TMJ can cause resistance to the bit, performance issues, decreased appetite, shortening of stride, hollow back, and uneven wearing of teeth.

When people force themselves to smile even when they aren't happy, it can make them feel happier simply by pretending. Physical displays of emotion can make you feel the emotion even if you didn't start out feeling that way.

Emotional stress in humans causes us to tighten our neck muscles and clench our jaws. Horses experience a similar response.

If a whorl, or whorls, on a horse's cheek causes them to keep their jaw clenched, it can cause the horse to feel stressed, the same way a fake smile can make us feel happy. Without assistance to loosen their jaw muscles and relax, this muscle tension can cause an anxious horse who tends to worry.

It is easy to see how a cheek whorl could have been considered bad luck. With the benefits of a modern viewpoint, we can look at the possibility of bad teeth causing pain and difficulty in maintaining proper nutrition. This can cause a horse to have trouble holding weight or doing a full days work. It can also cause a stressed horse who, with rough handling, could explode when pressured.

With an understanding of the pain throughout the entire body brought on by an inflamed TMJ, it is easy to see why these horses could have been considered bad luck.

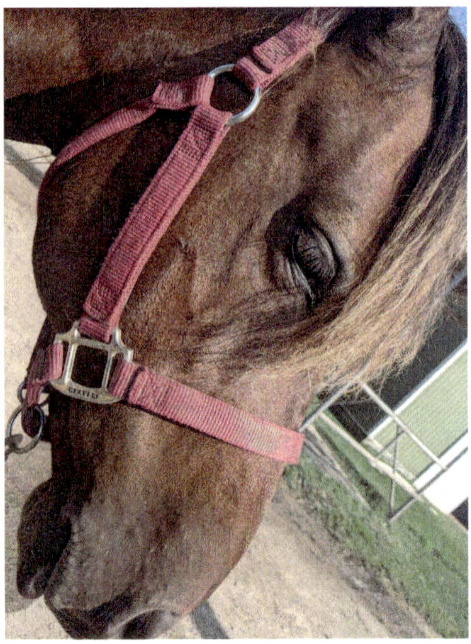

When your livelihood is dependent on your horse's ability to work, a horse with bad teeth would indeed be bad luck. With modern dental practices, teeth abnormalities can be easily cared for and this is no longer a sign of ruin.

Of course, a horse can also have problems with their TMJ brought on by other causes such as trauma, bit pain, incorrect balance in the feet, and poor saddle fit. There doesn't have to be a whorl for there to be problems and not all horses with cheek whorls will be stressed or have uneven teeth.

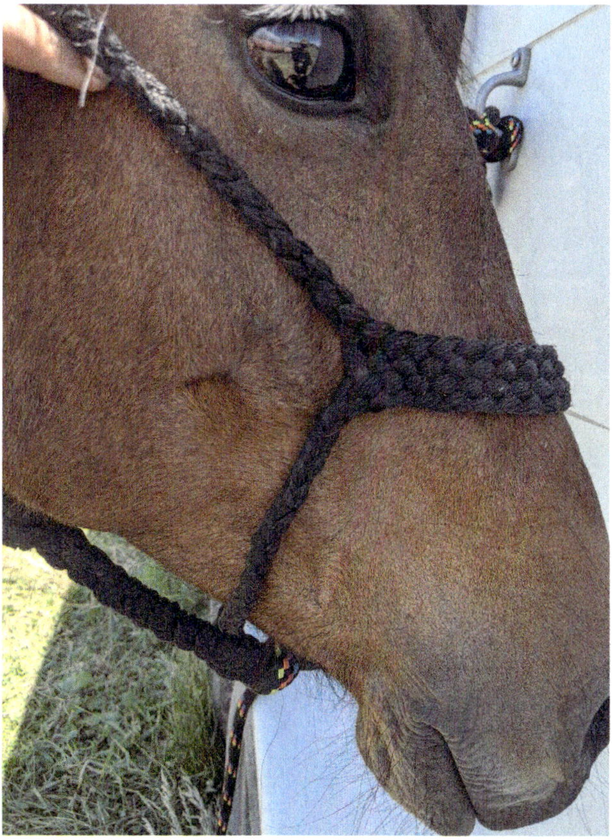

Often horses will have both jaw and cheek whorls. This creates a combination of the results we would expect to see from each one individually.

Jaw Whorls

Jaw whorls are different than cheek whorls in many ways. They don't appear to cause as much stress. Instead, all the horses I have come across with jaw whorls are left-brained extroverts.
Far from a horse who is stressed, they show a horse who is calm, curious, and confident.

Temple Whorls

Whorls on the temples are said to show a horse who is an exceptionally quick thinker. They can think up ways to keep themselves entertained and all sorts of good ways to get into trouble. Being fast learners, they may learn lessons that were not what you intended to teach. A person has to be on top of their game to keep up with an animal with these whorls when training.

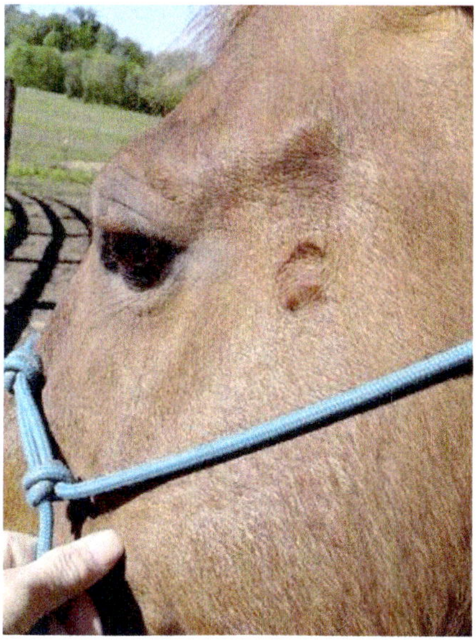

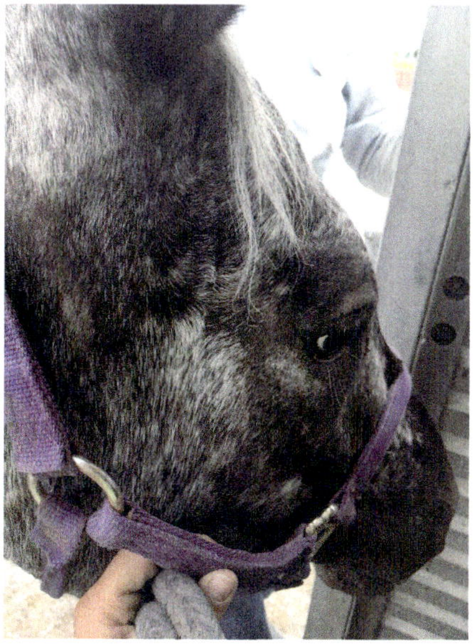

Temple whorls can be set above or below the eye and still hold the same meaning. Both of these animals are very quick learners and eager to work.

Mustache

Mustaches are most common in breeds of horses that have a lot of other body hair, such as feathering around the legs and very full manes. Not surprisingly, these are usually draft breeds.

Draft breeds are known for their even temperament and docile ways. So it shouldn't come as a surprise that a mustache is supposed to show a horse who is docile and even-tempered.

Other breeds can have mustaches too, of course! The meaning is still the same.

Mustaches can vary from a slight bit of extra hair on the upper lip to a full robust growth of hair that would make any man proud.

It is said that mustaches on horses indicate a "babysitter." They seem to know the riders' capabilities and behave accordingly. They take care of their rider, but teach them as well. The more capable of a rider the horse thinks you are, the more challenging it acts, keeping you safe all the while.

Unknown Whorls

Despite how much we can learn by looking at a horse's whorls, there is still so much we don't know!

We know that uniformity matters, and it does make a difference in the whorls all horses have along the bottom of their jaws. Unmatched whorls there make for unevenness, just like in the rest of the body. The shape and size differ greatly, and we don't know what the different patterns mean. The same applies to whorls under a horse's stomach. They vary from long and feathered to small and tight. Although all horses have whorls in these places, we don't know what they mean.

Then there are the odd and unique whorls that pop up in random places across a horse's body.

While we have an idea that these whorls will affect that area in some way, we don't know exactly how or why.

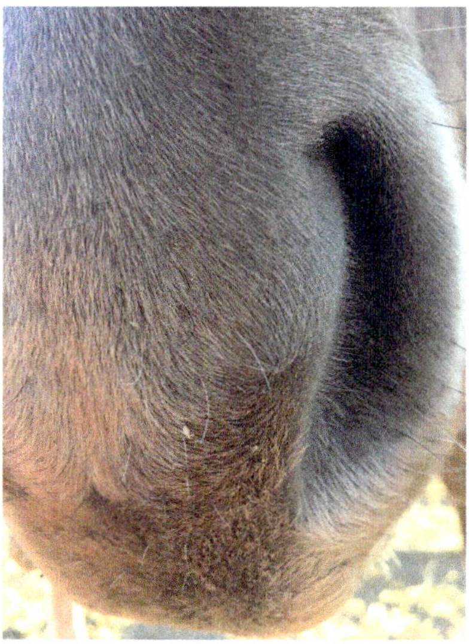

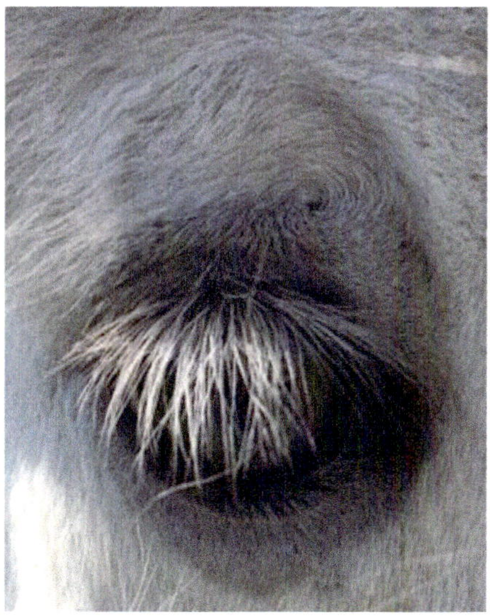

Forelock Whorls

When looking at the whorls on a horse's head, it is easy to get confused by the forelock whorls. All horses have a whorl at the base of their forelock. These whorls can vary from being barely there to having large and intricate designs. These whorls do not count though, when we are looking at the the amount or placement of whorls on the forehead.

I have heard it said that the direction hair swirls in this whorl is a stronger indicator of sidedness than any other whorl on a horse. Other than that possibility, we don't know the meaning of this whorl. Someday these whorls will probably be able to give us more clues about temperament, but not yet.

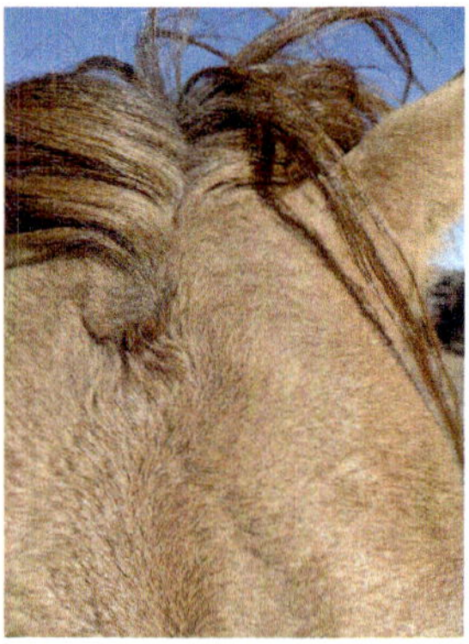

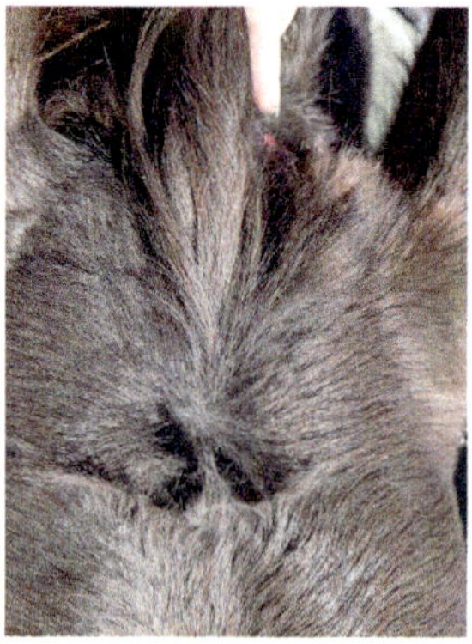

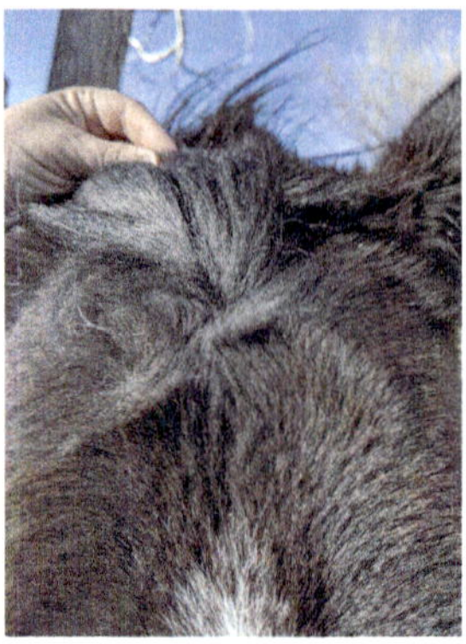

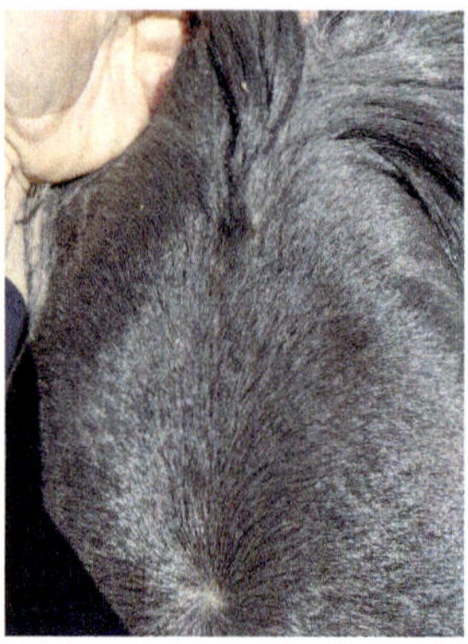

Double Whorls

More than one whorl means the horse will show more than one of the four personality traits.

Often these can be opposite traits. A horse with a high whorl and a low whorl will be an energetic extrovert sometimes and a calm, easy-going introvert other times. The difference can be a bit shocking, leading to the saying that they have double personalities.

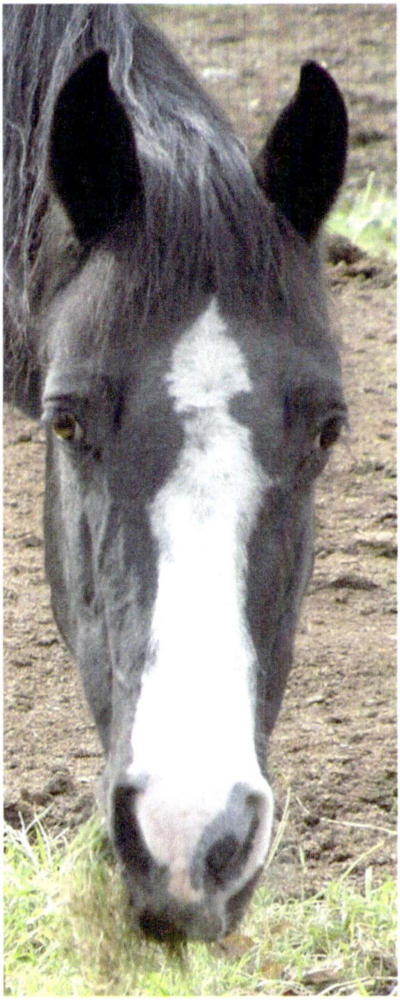

High Side By Side Double Whorls

A horse with two high tight whorls side by side is both left and right-brain. They seem to possess an ability to hyperfocus. Tough, smart, and intent on their job, they are a super power in the right hands. Although these horses are bold and brave, they are also sensitive enough that riders who don't acknowledge their superior intellect can offend them and have a fight on their hands.

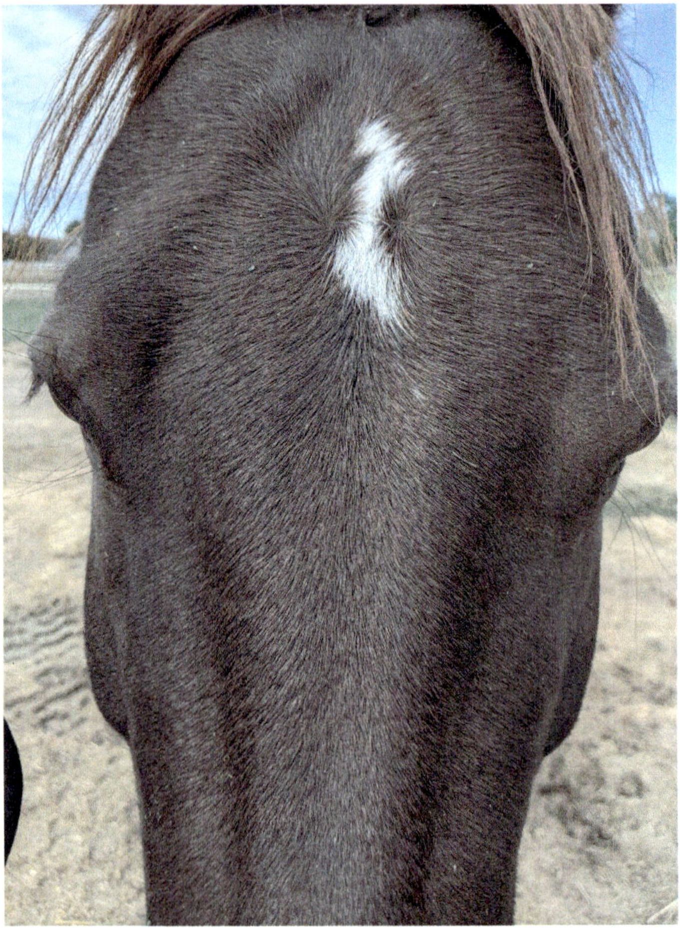

Stacked Double Whorl

A stacked double whorl includes two whorls, one above the other. Having both introvert and extrovert qualities, these horses can be quiet and disinterested one minute and over energetic, in your face the next. While they may have a bit of a bad reputation, stacked double whorls are capable of being wonderful horses. Their changes in temperament can keep life interesting, and they are willing trustworthy mounts.

They just can't be handled roughly. Horses with a single whorl might let you get away with being a poor rider, but double whorls demand fair and kind treatment.

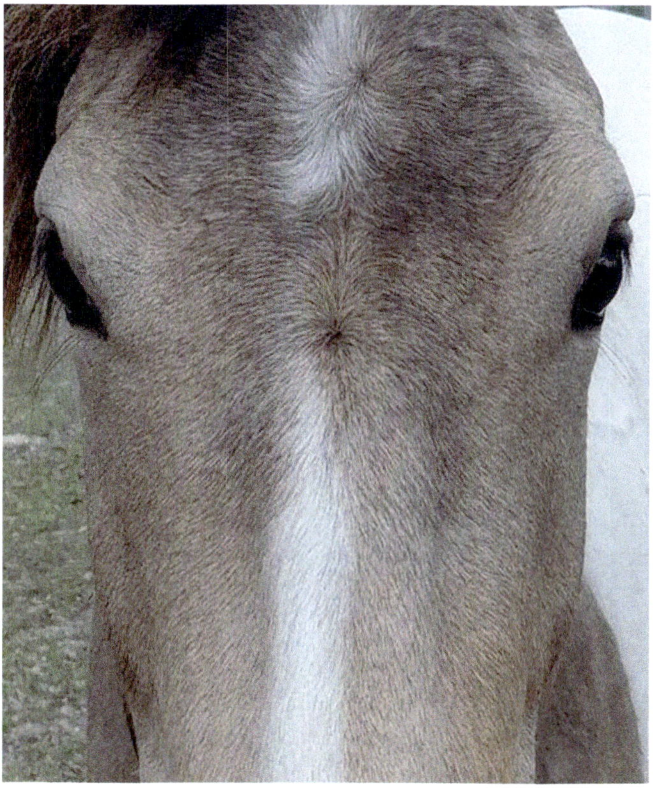

A Center Whorl With An Outlier

Another fairly common whorl pattern is a single-center whorl with a second whorl positioned high on the forehead and off to the right or left side of the head.

Horses with these whorls are mostly basic and simple. Except for those occasions where they show extreme right or left-brained extrovert behavior.

A horse with an outlier whorl to the right will be mostly quiet, except when they are extremely sensitive, reactive, and emotional.

A horse with an outlier to the left will be pretty basic and occasionally extremely bold and brave.

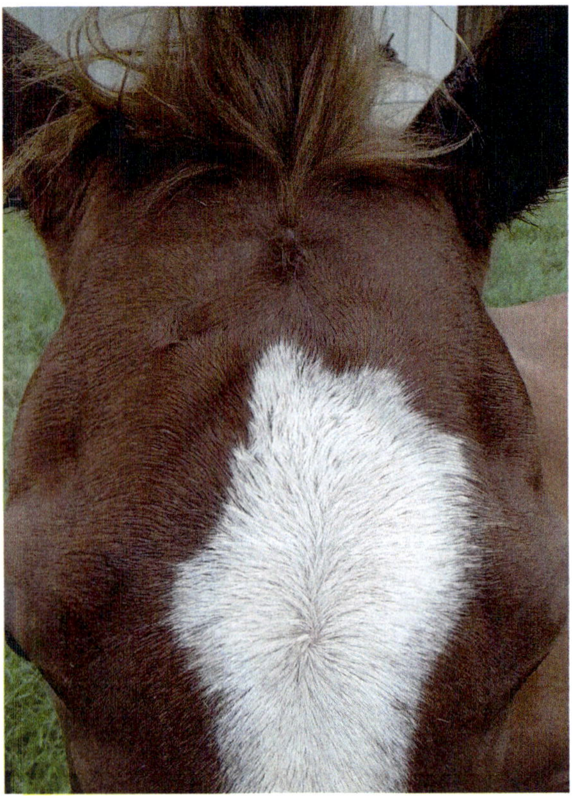

Diagonal Whorls

Side by side at a slant, diagonal whorls aren't all that different from a simple side-by-side whorl, and it can be difficult to tell the difference. They are positioned at an angle and are a slight distance apart. This is not to be confused with a single whorl with an outlier where the whorls are farther apart, and there is usually faint feathering that connects them. Plain side-by-side double whorls can sit at a slight slant, but without the space and feathering they are still only side-by-side whorls.

Sometimes known as a Z pattern. These horses have been said to be unpredictable, dangerous, and protective of their personal space with a tendency to explode if pushed.

I have found that these horses tend to be introverts, usually right brain introverts, even when the whorls are high, as they usually are. They are commonly quiet and withdrawn. Then, when pushed too far because people failed to notice their minimal display of emotion, they will explode in a manner that seems to be out of nowhere.

Introverts need to feel safe. Very sensitive to pressure, these horses will shut down when under stress. They don't want to move their feet, but that doesn't mean they aren't thinking. They just take longer for the thought to be acted on and need patience to avoid upsetting them.

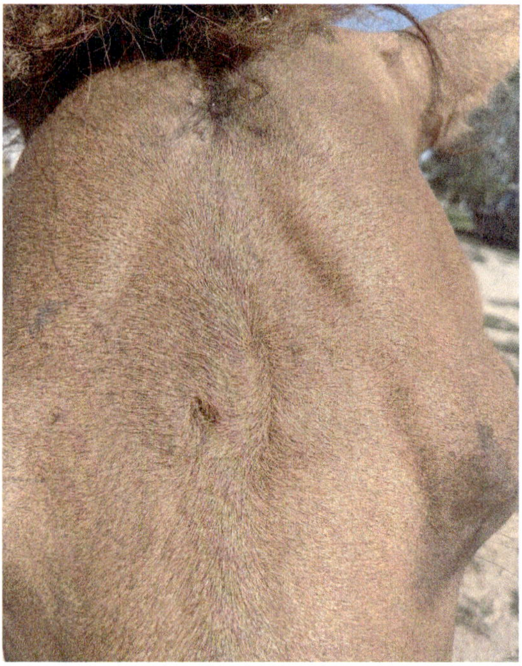

Although the second whorl is faint on this horse, it is still there, low and to our left. There is the typical space between the whorls, as well as the feathering looping between the two diagonal whorls.

Low Side By Side Double Whorl

Unlike a high side-by-side double whorl, double whorls placed low on the head seem to show a predominantly left-brained horse. Being very quick learners, they can grasp a new lesson almost immediately.

Covering the entire range of the left brain, they are both introverted and extroverted. While calm and confident, they are also playful, curious, and friendly.

Multiple Whorls

We don't hear much about the meaning of more than two whorls and what we usually hear is that they are "complicated."

That may be true, but like horses with with one or two whorls, the position of the larger number of whorls can have great influence on the exact meaning.

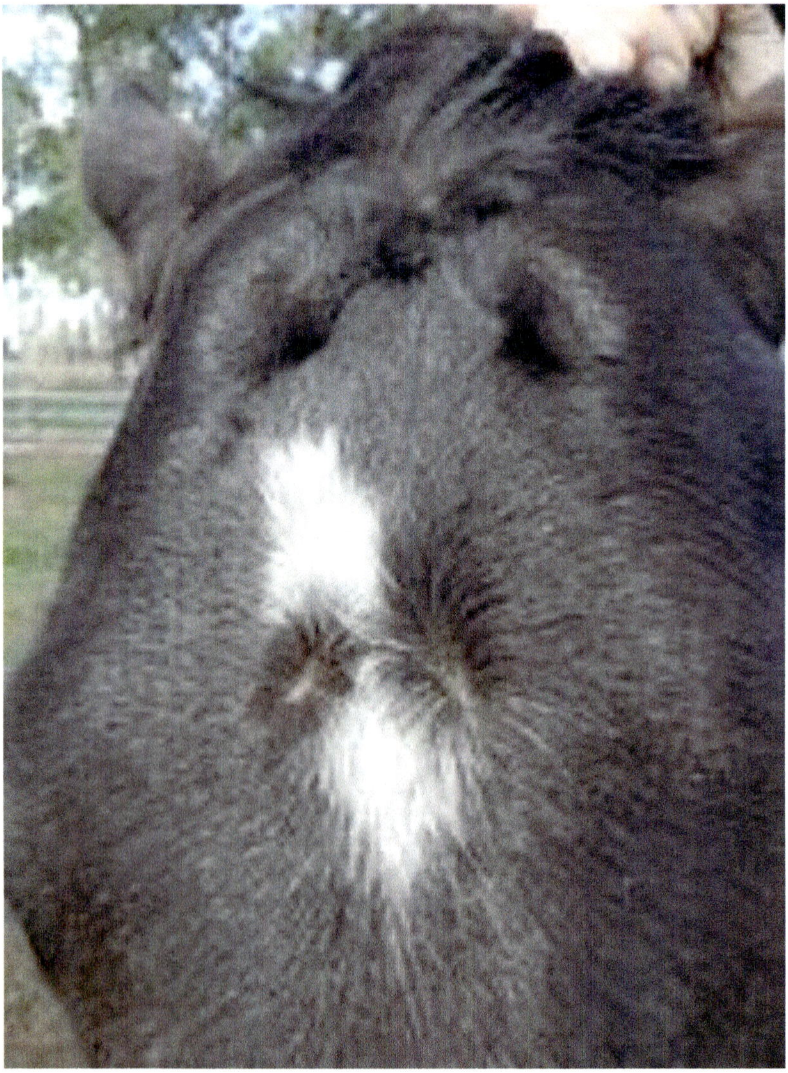

Three Whorls

Three whorls will often come in a triangle pattern, with two high whorls on either side of the forelock and in the center between the eyes. They can come in almost any pattern though, and the location of the whorl doesn't matter as much as the number. Three whorls in a straight line is a seperate pattern and falls differently into this category.

Without fail, my research has shown that the owners of horses with this whorl pattern have classified them as left-brained extroverts, calm, steady, very smart, willing, and eager to learn. Their owners love them and, other than admitting that they can be quite quirky, had no complaints.

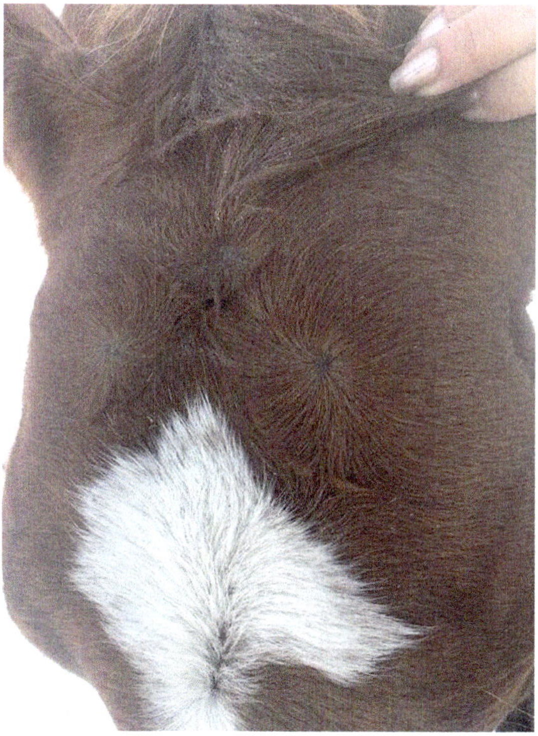

The typical 'triangle' pattern with two high whorls and a single center at the base.

Studs carrying this whorl are traditionally said to be dangerous, but with no examples to judge from, that could be no more than superstition. Excessively smart horses have been confounding riders who aren't as smart as their horses for as long as horses have been ridden. It is possible that the reputation of complicated and dangerous traits in studs with three whorls was created by people who tried to force these horses into submission and came out on the losing end.

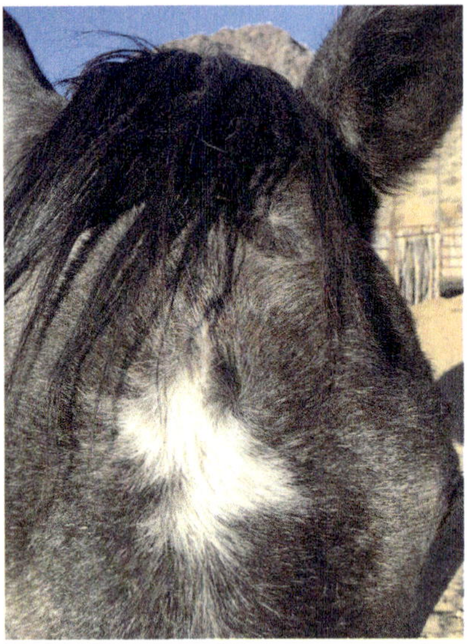

At first glance, this horse appears to have a diagonal double, but closer inspection shows an outlier whorl. Despite the unusual placement of his three whorls he still displays the super gentle, easy going temperament we would expect from these whorls. Not the occasional extreme right brain behavior the outlier would usually cause or the introverted behavior the diagonal doubles would lead us to expect.

This horse's whorl is set the opposite way. Two center whorls set close together and a high left outlier. Sensitive, smart, and confident, she does occasionally get quite hot.

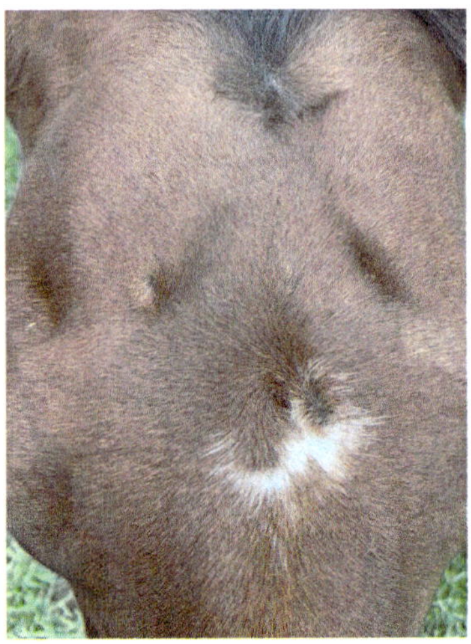

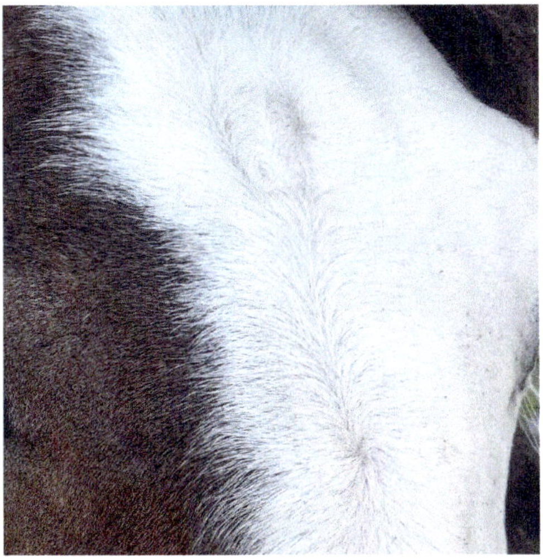

These horses display three whorls in the triangle pattern but with lots of feathering. The feathering amplifies the left brain tendencies, more friendly, more bold, more brave.

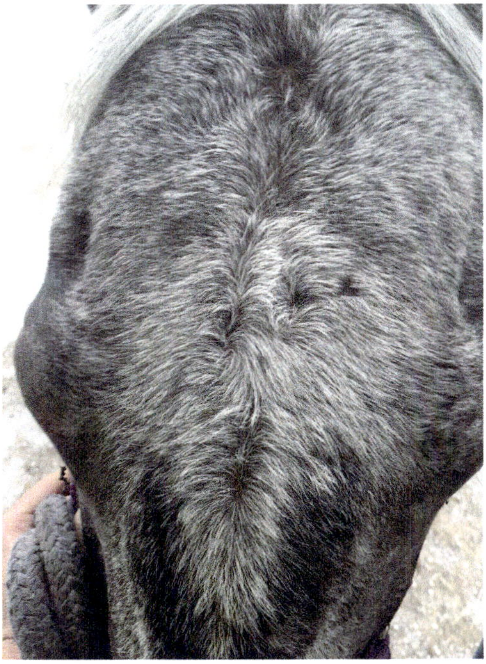

When the three whorls are in a line instead of a triangle, the horse will be more energetic and NOT the born broke type. They are still left brain extroverts, just with a lot more energy.

Four Whorls

With three whorls, we get a left-brained horse. With four whorls, we seem to end up with a right-brained horse. Two sets of double whorls above the eyes in a square pattern appears to produce a horse who is ridiculously smart and occasionally aggressive.

Knowing if the occasional aggressive tendencies come from the whorl type or bad handling can be hard to tell. Bad handling can produce problems in any extremely intelligent, emotional, and reactive horse. More so than in one who is more willing to go quietly along with whatever is asked of them without thinking so hard about it.

All horses should be trained with kindness and patience, but these horses demand it; otherwise, the results will be disastrous.

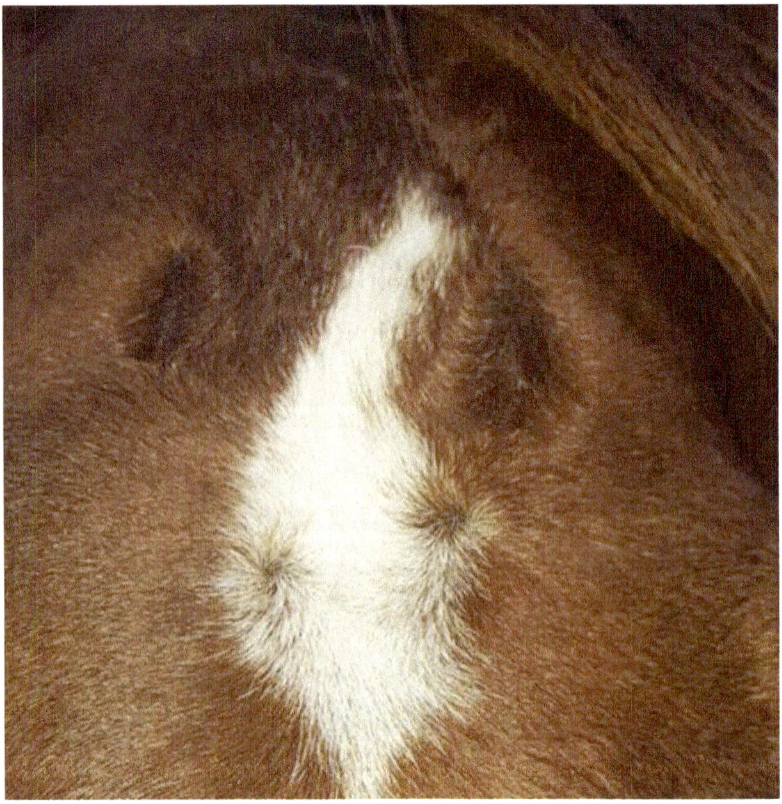

Five Or More Whorls

As we get into higher number of whorls there aren't enough examples to get exact ideas of the meanings. Often, they are introverts instead of extroverts, and they can be left or right-brained.

What they do have in common is that they are very complicated. Sensitive, spirited, and incredibly smart, they need a rider who can keep up with them. When treated roughly, they can be volatile and reactive. They will try their hardest once they feel understood and heard, but they will always demand fair treatment and respect. They are commonly a one-person horse and, once they have a relationship with that person, together they can accomplish anything.

Although horses with large numbers of whorls can be intimidating at first, for a confident rider, they are well worth working through the difficulties to find the gold underneath.

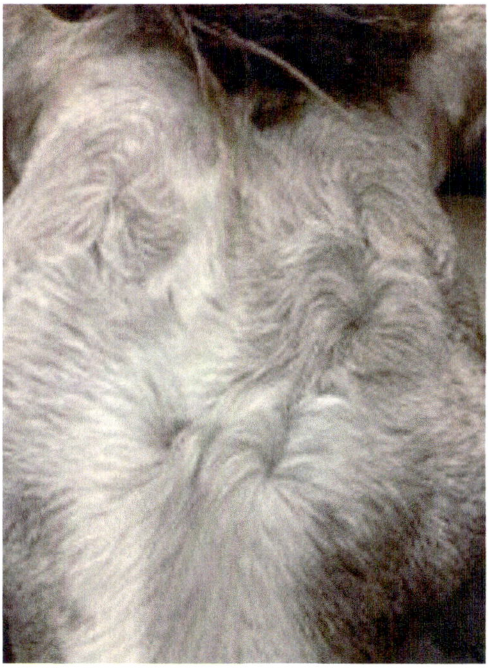

A young filly who was in training to ride at the time of this picture. She was doing extremely well with a quiet and agreeable temperament.

Body Whorls

Whorls on different body parts can tell us about what is going on inside the horse too.

A whorl on one side that isn't matched on the other side shows a horse that isn't even from side to side, no matter what part of the body the whorl is on. There will often be a strong preference for the side with the whorl as far as leads and curving their body. Bending away from the whorl is difficult when there is an unmatched whorl.

Depending on placement and size, uneven whorls can lead to major imbalances. I knew a horse once who had completely unmatched flank whorls. One nearly reached his back bone, the other was very short. He was never able to control his body, and riding further unbalanced him. The lack of stability left him scared and prone to sudden bolts when ridden.

A horse will push into big splaying whorls. If one side of the body has a small whorl and the other has a big splaying whorl, it will intensify the curving effect and lead to issues with the body that make training difficult.

Throatlatch

All horses have whorls in the throatlatch area.

Some throatlatch whorls will be bigger than others. The larger the whorls are, the less willing the horse will be to tuck their head down to, or behind, the vertical. This is not entirely a bad thing since behind the vertical is not desired in training.

A horse with large whorls around their throatlatch will want to carry their head forward and up. They will often have a little extra muscling on the bottom side of the neck.

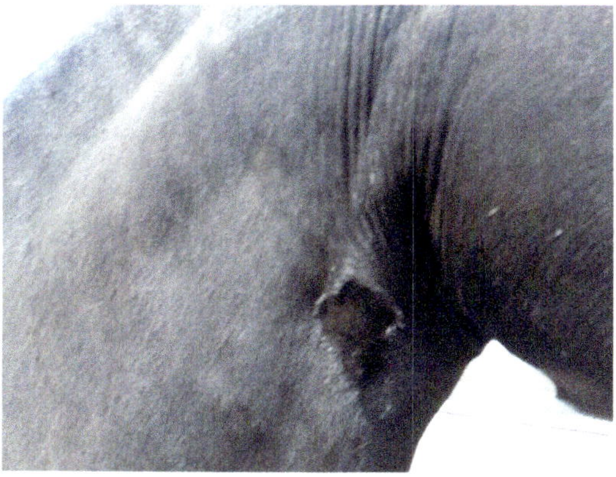

Large whorls in the throatlatch area cause a horse to resist tucking their head and to have extra muscling under the neck.

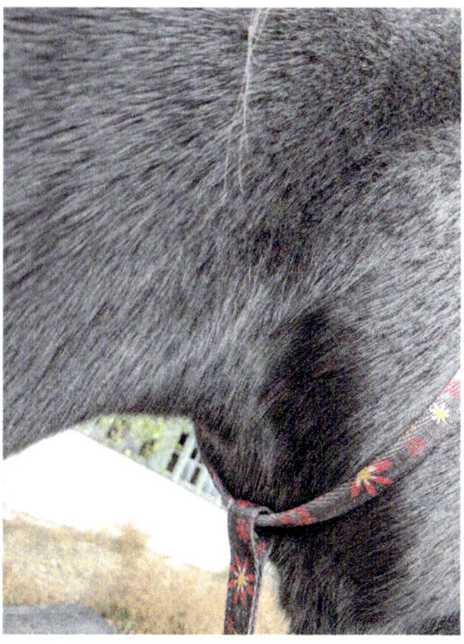

This horse has almost nonexistent whorls in the throatlatch area. He likes to tuck his head, and has little to no muscling under the neck.

Neck Whorls, On The Crest

A whorl on the crest of the neck will show where a horse will want to bend through the neck. When the whorls are directly behind the ears they will bend evenly throughout the neck.

In a horse with a whorl halfway down the neck on the crest, you will usually see a high point in the crest directly over the whorl. Often it will be in the place where the mane switches sides.

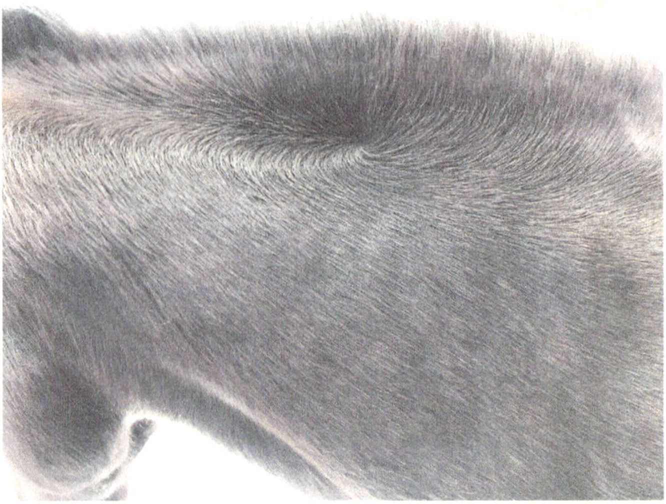

If there is a whorl on one side of the neck but not the other, the horse will want to bend the neck around the whorl. It isn't necessarily a hindrance to training unless it is extreme, but it can help to be aware.

Instead of bending at one point, horses with feathered whorls bend their necks through the length of the feathering. As long as there is feathering on both sides of the neck, it creates a very supple neck that rounds naturally.

A feathered whorl down the crest of the neck seems to affect balance when there is only one side with feathering. These whorls can throw a horse onto the forehand making them heavier on the front leg of the side with the whorl.

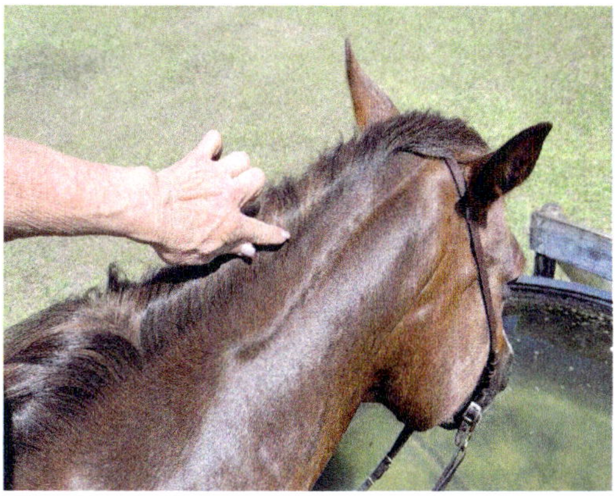

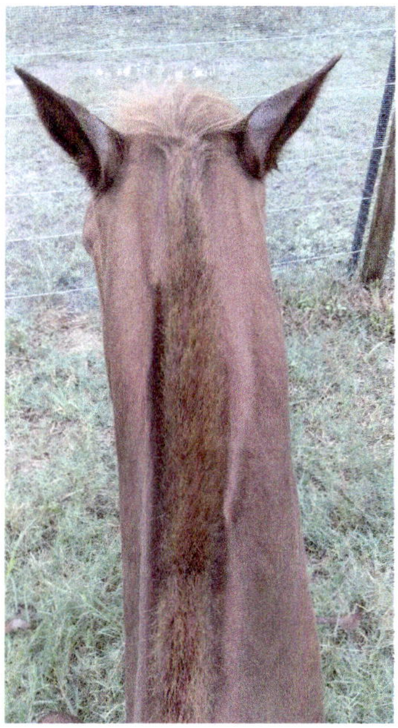

Feathering can come in all different lengths and locations on the neck.

Neck Whorls, On The Base

A whorl on the front of the neck will usually mean the horse will carry some extra muscling in that area of the neck, even with correct riding. The horse will tend to carry their neck straight in the place with the whorl. The neck will want to round over the whorl.

When a horse has a big open splaying whorl on the front of the neck, or the shredded wheat pattern said to be bad luck in old superstition, they will push against it with the rest of their body. This often results in a horse with a ewe neck. When the whorl extends down through the chest, it will pull the horse heavily onto the forehand.

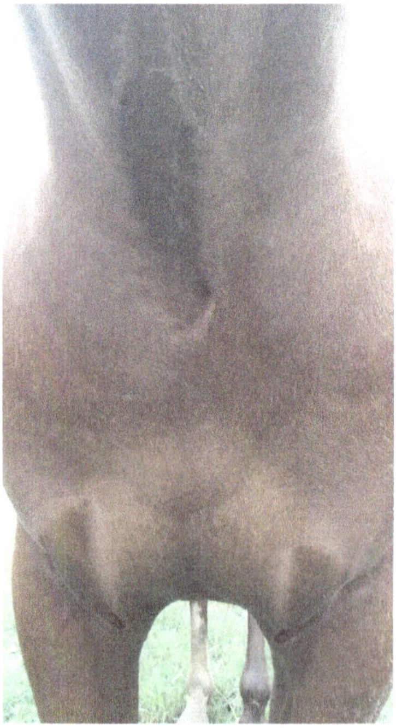

A large open splaying whorl leads to an upside down neck and a horse who is heavy on the forehand.

A smaller whorl causes this horse to be upright through the base of the neck, where the whorl is, and to round his neck over the whorl.

A zipper whorl, where the hair comes together forming a ridge in the center, is different than an open splaying whorl. Instead of showing a horse who is heavy on the forehand, it is a sign of high head carriage. The horse will be very upright through the neck in the location of the whorl but not ewe necked. The neck will arch nicely over it instead of pushing down into the whorl. It accompanies a horse who is light on the forehand.

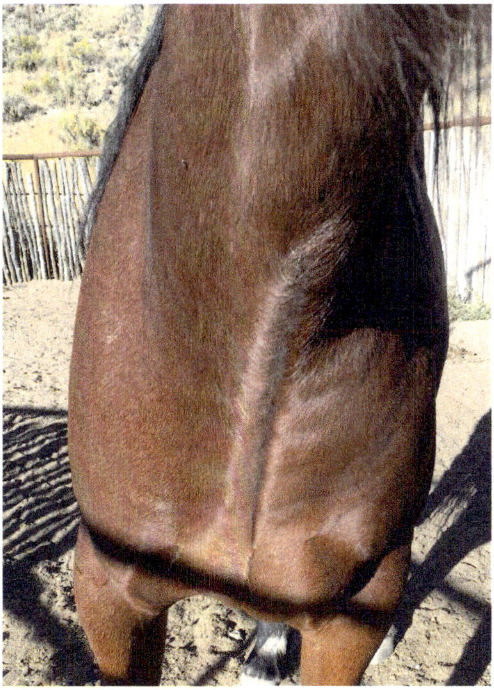

With a combination of whorls on the neck, you can get a mix of traits. A small whorl, as this horse has below the throatlatch, will cause a horse to bend around it. An open splaying whorl, low on the neck here and to the right, will cause them to push into, and curve away from it.
When the two types are opposite, they will amplify the effect of each other. This horse will be heavy on her right front and want to carry her head to the left.

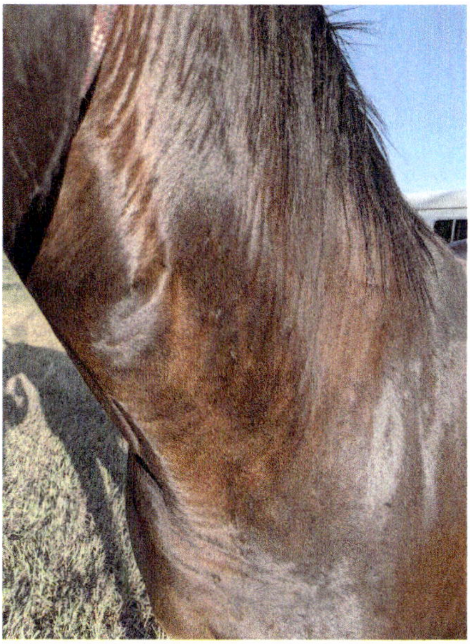

Neck Whorls, On The Side

Large whorls on the side of the neck tend to make the neck bend easily from side to side. How these whorls make the neck bend depends on the type of whorl.

A small tight whorl with lines of feathering coming off of it makes the horse bend around the whorl.

Large open splaying whorls can occur on the side of the neck as well as on the bottom. As with anywhere else, open splaying whorls cause the muscle to bulge there and bend away from the whorl. Unfortunately, it can sometimes be hard to tell the difference.

When the whorls are on both sides, the neck will be extremely supple.

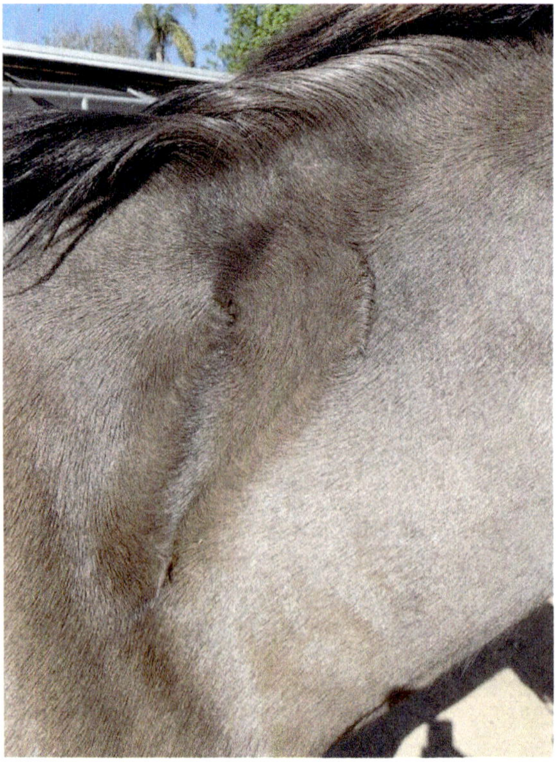

The large whorls on this side of this horse's neck, without matching whorls on the opposite side, mean that he will turn more easily in the direction of the whorls. This is also the direction that the mane lays. He should be soft to the right and stiff when going to the left.

Chest Whorls

Normal chest whorls are two evenly sized feathered whorls coming up the pectoral muscles where each front leg meets the chest. When these whorls are short, the horse will have short reach and low leg action with the front legs. When these whorls stretch high up onto the chest, the leg action will be higher.

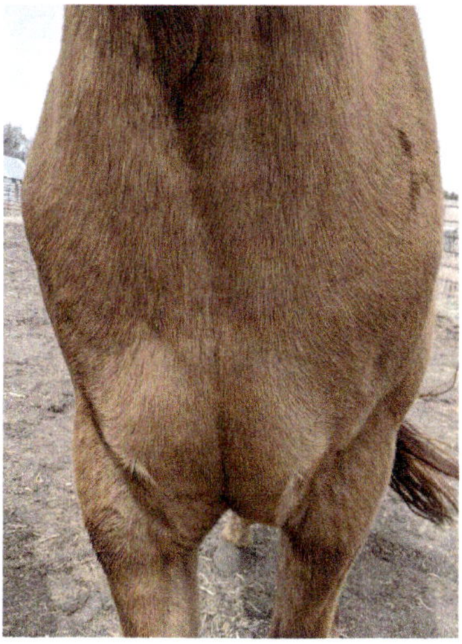

This horse has very average chest whorls. They are matched but don't reach very high into the chest. No other whorls on this chest. All very normal and even.

When there is a whorl off to one side of the chest, there will be a preference for the lead on that side of the body, depending on what type of whorl it is.

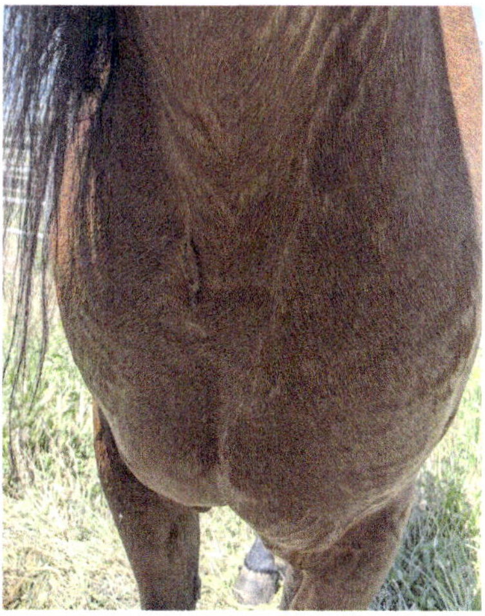

This horse has a feathered whorl on the right side of the chest. That means the muscles will be tighter in that area, leading to slight gait unevenness.

Most whorls in the center of the chest show a horse whose neck will be low and heavy. This is true whether it's a whorl in the center of the chest or a long whorl that starts on the neck and comes down well into the chest.

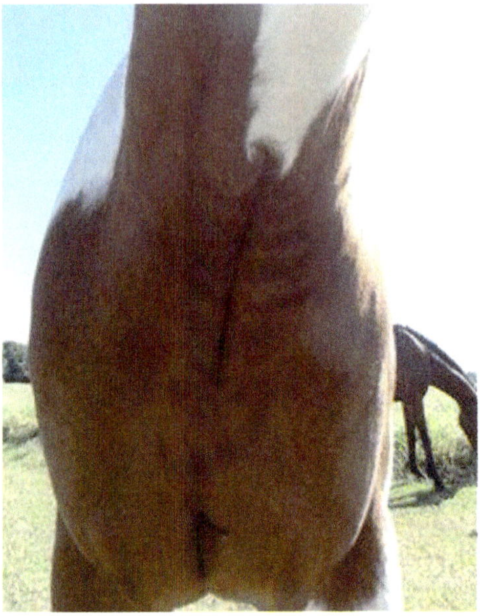

The types of whorls make a big difference. This horse has a zipper whorl coming down from the neck and a separate lower whorl. This zipper whorl means the neck will be heavy on the base but arch over the whorl. The separate whorl low on the chest emphasizes the low headset. The whorls on the pectorals are small, suggesting he will have low sweeping leg action.

Although the neck and chest whorls on both of these horses are somewhat similar, they will have very different conformation and head carriage. Without the lower whorl in the center of the chest, this horse's neck will be carried higher. The long exaggerated whorls on the pectorals will cause high forward leg action.

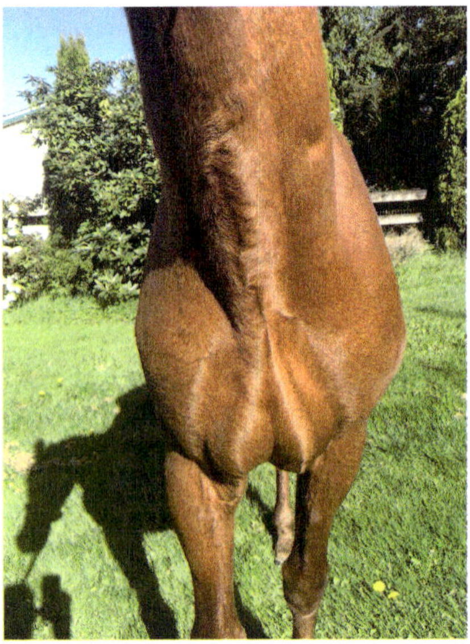

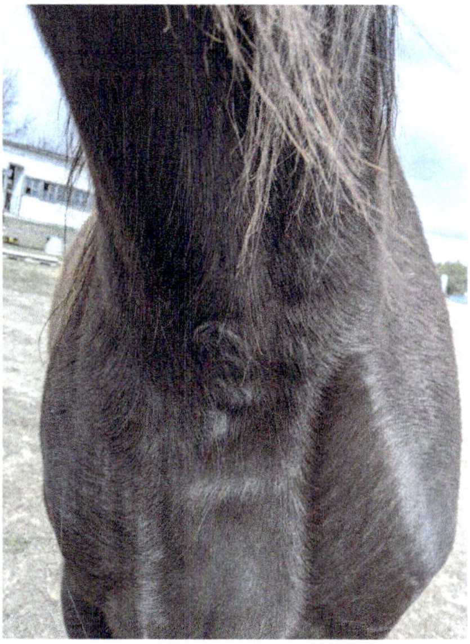

With large unbalanced feathering on one side of the chest reaching to the neck this horse will have uneven movement and lead preferences. He likes to use the leg with extra feathering the same way a dog does, reaching and pawing with it.

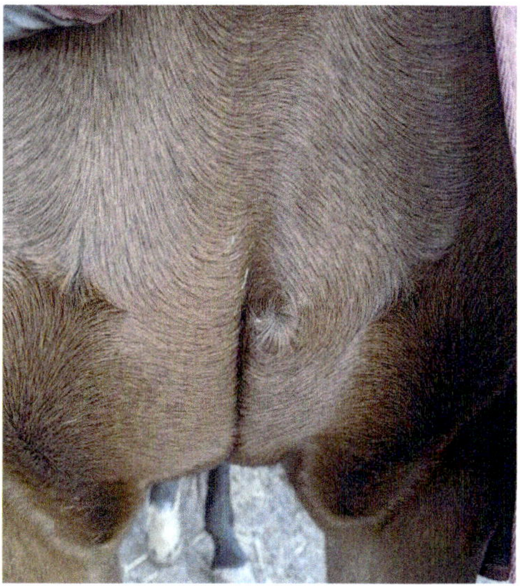

A single whorl in the center of the chest accompanies a low heavy neck set.

Neck And Chest Whorls

It is easy to describe how neck and chest whorls will affect a headset, but it can be clearer to distinguish them in photos. These horses are examples of very different or even slightly similar neck and chest whorls. They show the effects these whorls have on conformation.

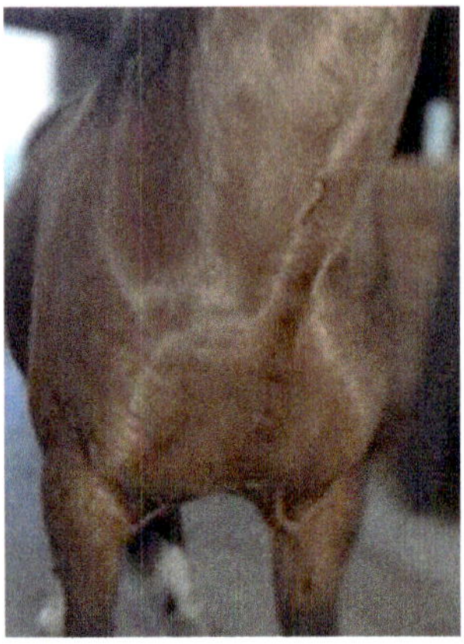

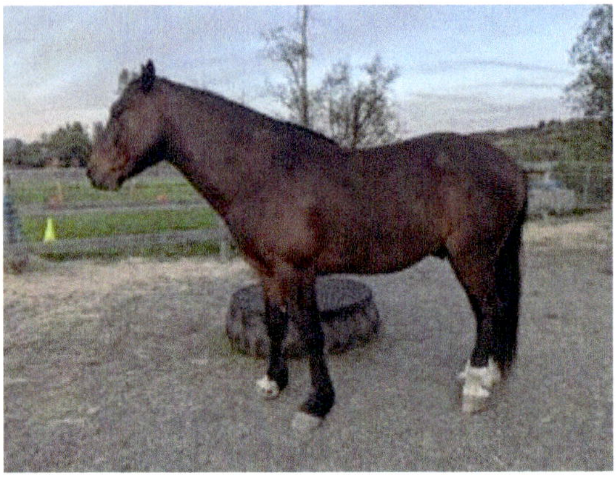

Both of these horses have open splaying whorls down the base of their necks. The hair covering the entire chest of the top horse is a whorl, it grows upwards instead of down, the whorl up the base of the neck stops at the chest. The bottom horse has a neck whorl that goes all the way down the chest. The similar whorls create very different necks.

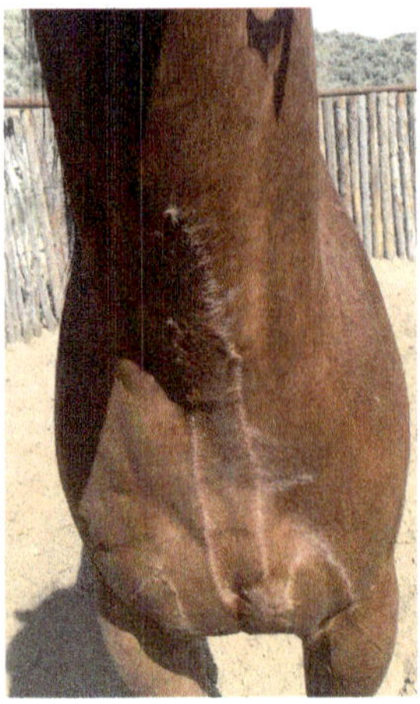

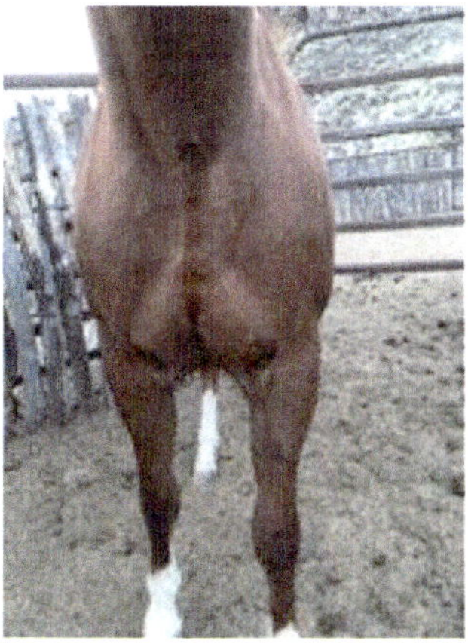

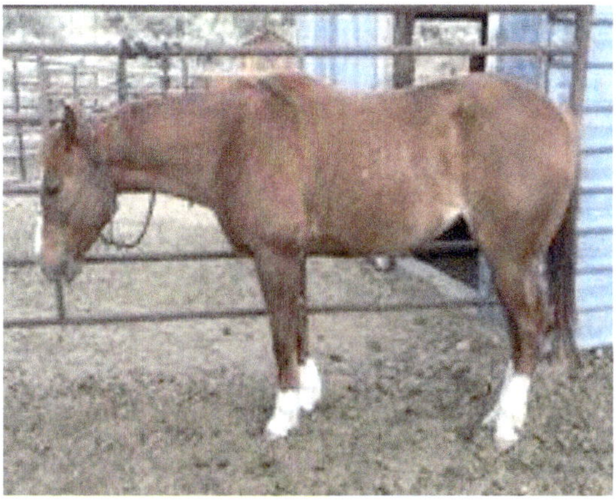

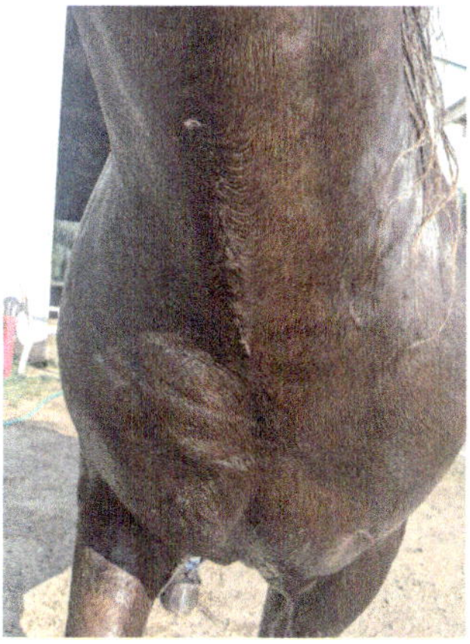

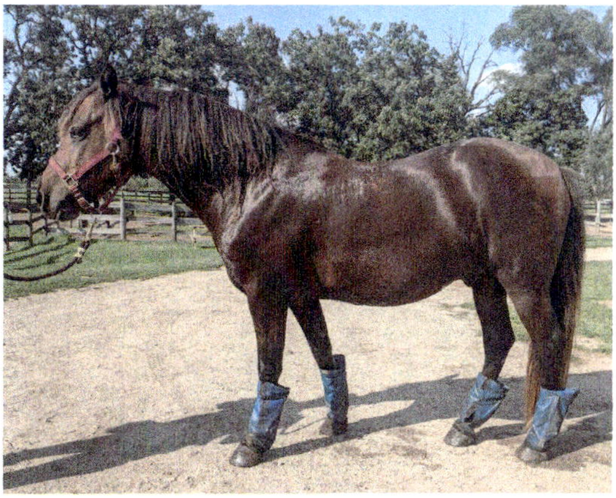

These horses have similar zipper-type whorls down their necks. The top horse's zipper whorl extends from the neck to the base of the chest. She has a much lower headset and carriage on a nicely muscled neck.

The bottom horse's zipper whorl is only at the base of the neck and does not extend into the chest. He has high head carriage with a more pronounced arch to his well-muscled neck.

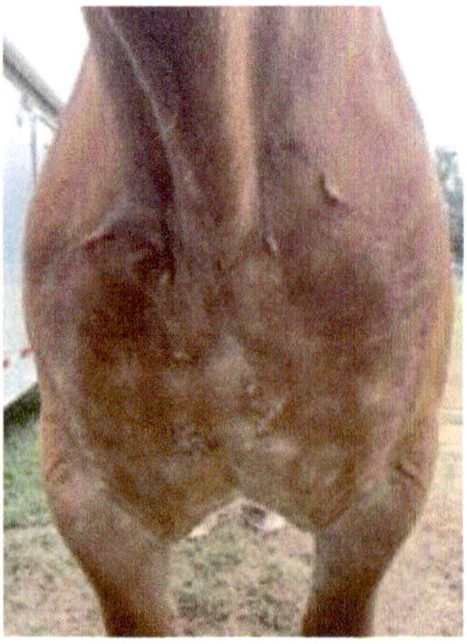

Usually a whorl on the chest shows a low thick neck. Both of these horses have whorls in different locations on the chest. They also both have zipper whorls. The shoulders are completely different but both have nicely set necks. The differences small changes in the whorls can make are amazing. There's an old cowboy saying about zipper whorls down the neck that "only a wealthy man can own such a horse." Horses with this marking, as long as there were no abnormal whorls, make sane, strong horses. Horses that only a wealthy man could afford.

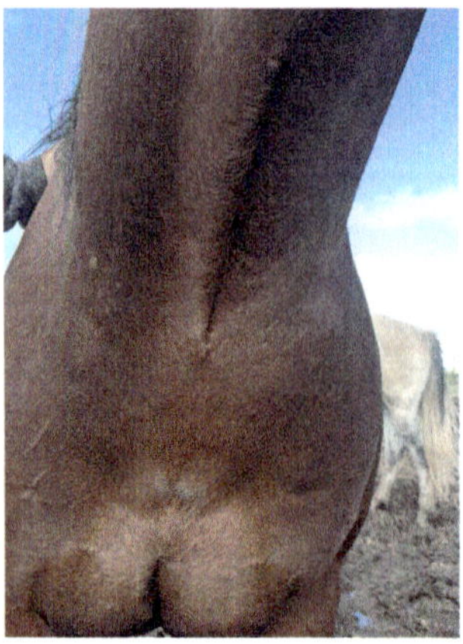

The Mane

Even a horse's mane has information to share.

The way a foal lies in utero affects the direction their mane falls toward. The side the mane falls on is the side a horse was curved to in the womb. It will also be the side that is easier for the horse to turn towards, initially at least.

When a young horse is first started under saddle, they may turn and pick up the lead easier to the side the mane falls on. Once training is well established, this side can become the weaker side that tends to be over bent and carried hollow.

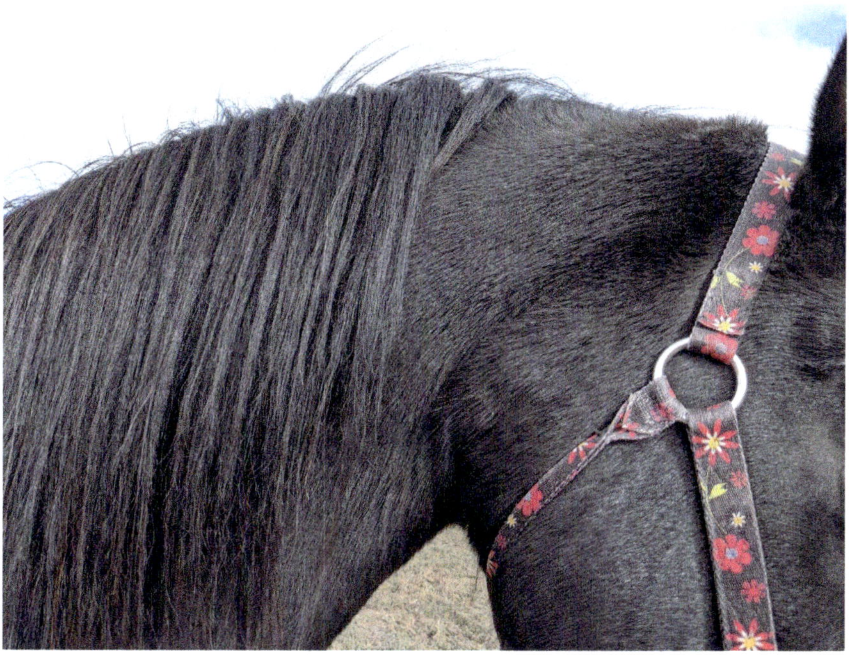

This horse has a swan neck, a neck set at a high upward angle with a tendency for the neck to arch while allowing the back to remain hollow. The mane switches sides at the exact location of the exaggerated bend of the neck.

When the mane is split down the middle and falls to both sides of the neck the horse is evenly developed on both sides. Unless it is due to an overwhelming amount of hair in the mane. Then it only means the horse is hairy.

A mane that changes sides part way down can be a sign of soreness or issues somewhere in the body. Often the change of sides will occur at a whorl. The place where the mane changes sides is significant too. Body work can often find sore spots that correlate with the mane switching sides. Or the position will be related to a conformational anomaly.

When parts of a horse's mane suddenly change sides, usually just a few strands, it is a sign of tension in the muscle along the top of the neck. This muscle is known as the trapezius cervicis, it is responsible for lifting scapula and raising the neck. Soreness in the neck can be fixed with bodywork such as massage and chiropractic adjustment, causing the mane to flip back to its original side.

A few strands of hair flipped to the wrong side of the neck can mean the wind is blowing, or that the horse is developing soreness.

The location of the split where a horse's mane switches sides can change or even disappear altogether with the mane going back to one side. When there are only a few hairs that switch sides, it is due to tension in the fascia. When it is the whole mane, it may have different causes.

Horses who go into training with large chunks of mane on opposite sides of the neck will often have it switch back, as training helps smooth out unevenness in the body.

The mental state of the horse seems to influence mane position too. Occasionally horses who haven't received bodywork or training can have their manes change seemingly only because of a change in circumstance, like going from a difficult life to a happier one.

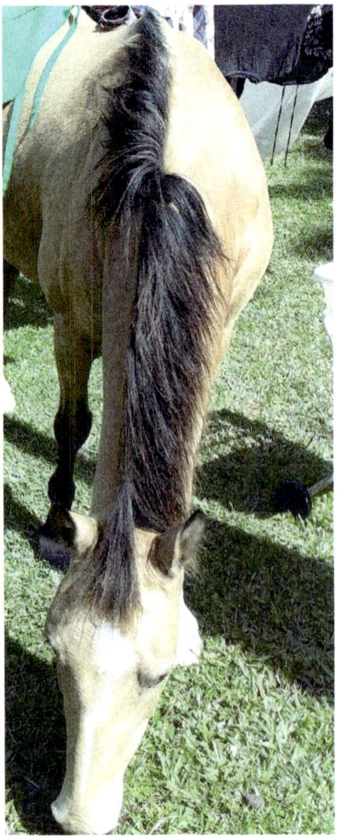

This mare's mane had always hung on different sides. She has a history of starvation and a large scar down her left shoulder that tells of a terrible injury. As she settled into a new home where she was happy and well-fed, the switch in the mane gradually moved lower and lower until it disappeared altogether, and now her mane only hangs on one side of the neck.

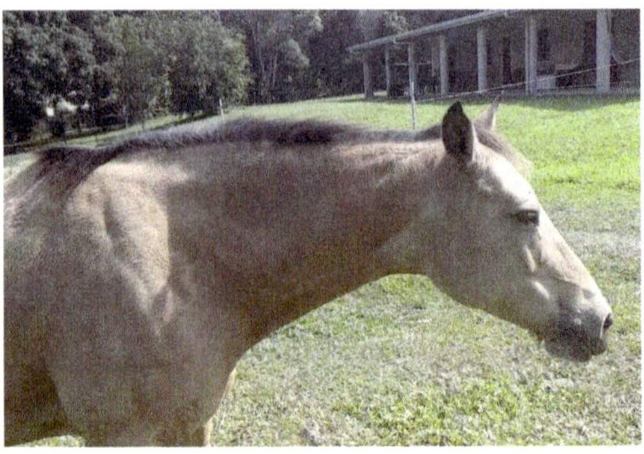

The thickness of the mane can give us clues to temperament too. Horses with thick full manes are usually quieter than horses with thin manes. This has to be taken in context, of course. A horse can have a thick mane and still have a thinner mane than other horses of the same breed.

Looking at the thickness of a mane is best applied when comparing two horses of the same basic type or looking at a horse with a simple whorl and trying to find more clues.

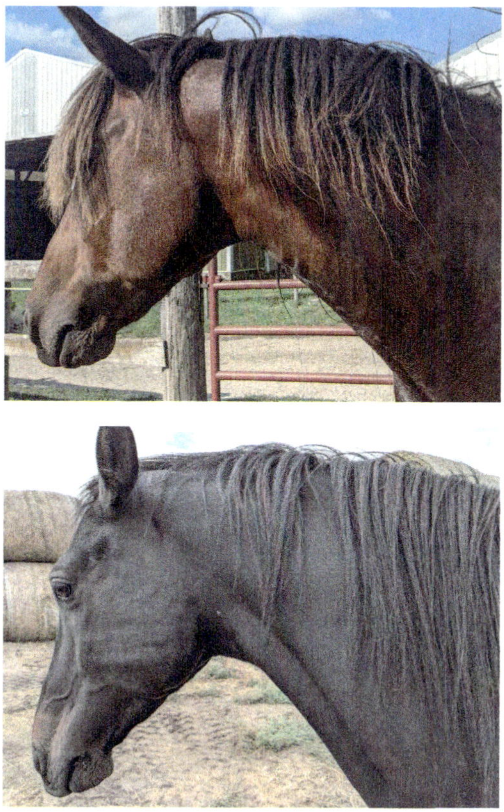

Two horses of the same age, breed, and whorl. The top horse has a very thick mane that splits in the middle and falls on both sides of the neck. The bottom horse has a fine thin mane.
Their temperaments are vastly different. One is a dependable riding horse, the other is extremely reactive and nervous.

Belly Whorls.

One place we don't think to look for whorls very often is under our horses' bellies. All horses have whorls there. The normal whorls would be one on either side of the center line. These whorls grow in opposite directions, one clockwise and one counter-clockwise, allowing the hair to lie in a uniform pattern on each side of the body.

The whorls on the underside of a horse's stomach can tell us how the horse will track with their hind legs. Matched whorls, placed in the same basic position on each side, show a horse who steps under himself evenly with each hind leg.

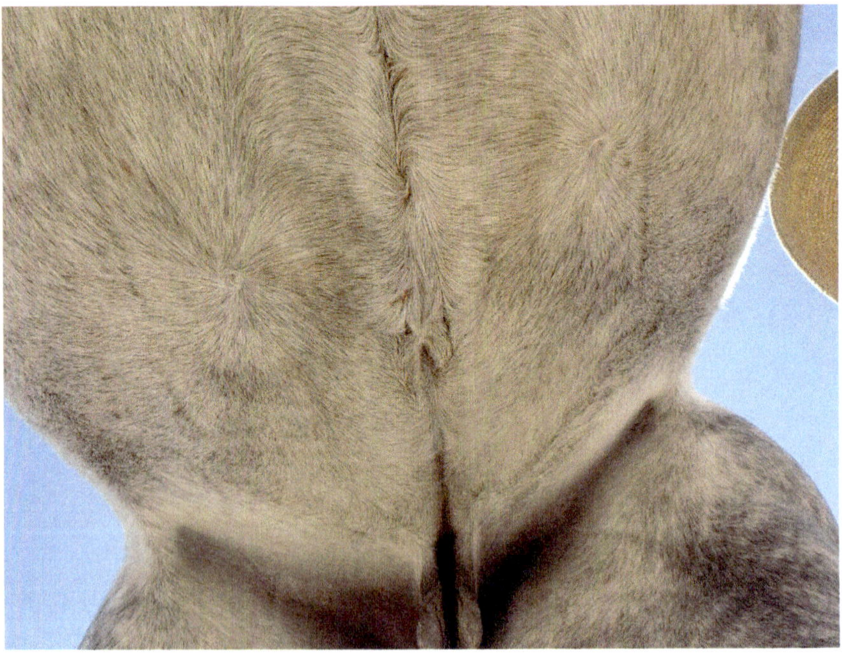

This horse prefers to push with her right hind leg, where the whorl is farther back, so she prefers her left lead.

A whorl towards the midline shows a horse who will step to the inside underneath himself. A whorl towards the outside of the belly shows a horse who swings their leg to the outside more before setting it down wide.

When one whorl is further forward than the other, the side with the farthest back whorl seems to be the stronger leg. The horse will tend to curve their body around the farther back whorl.

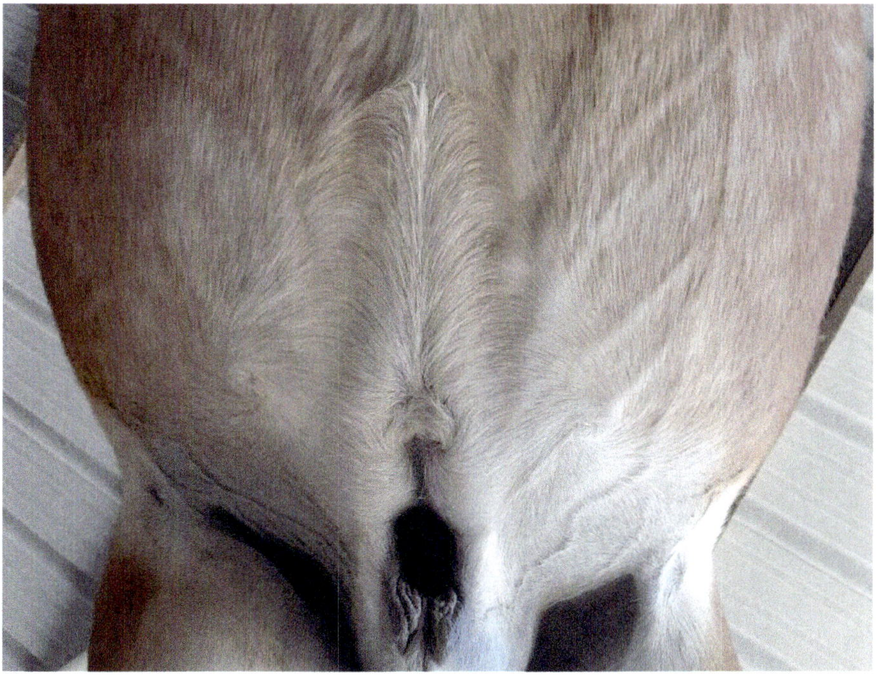

This horse's left hind leg tends to want to track closer to his midline and out behind him. His right hind is his preferred hind, so he prefers his left lead.

When the whorls are placed in a direct line between front and hind legs this allows them to step directly into the hoof print of the front hoof with the hind hoof. When a horse places their hind foot too far to the inside or outside, it may make it difficult for them to push off of it properly to create propulsion.

Horses also have a whorl down the center of their bellies. The meanings of these whorls are still completely unknown. There are a wide variety of whorl types and shapes that appear down the centerline of a horse's belly. They vary from small and round single whorls, to long feathered whorls. The long feathers seem to be most common.

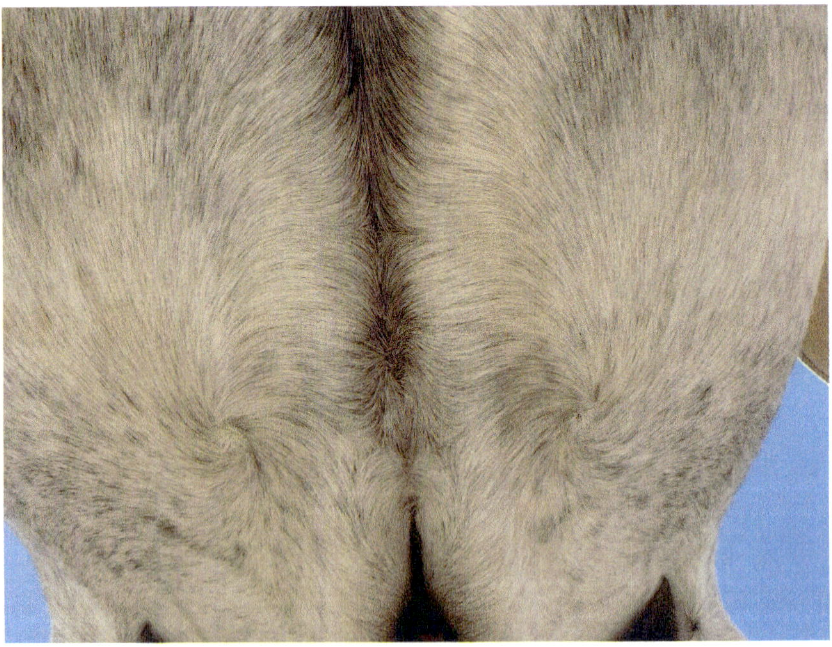

A feathered whorl down the center of the belly with side whorls placed towards the middle and rear. This horse will swing his hind legs towards the center and tends to trail his legs out behind.

Whorls On The Side Of The Belly

When a horse has whorls on the sides of their belly, just in front of the flanks, it is said that the whorls can show a tendency to carry some extra weight there. Mostly, it doesn't make a big difference in the horse's conformation and movement unless there is only a whorl on one side. With one belly whorl, they will curve more easily around it and be stiff when turning away from the whorl.

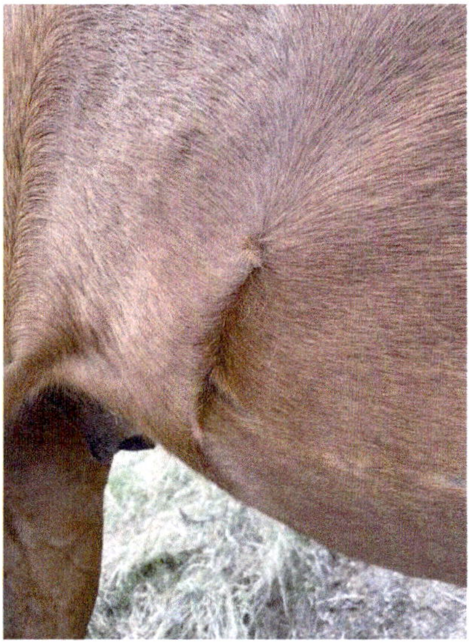

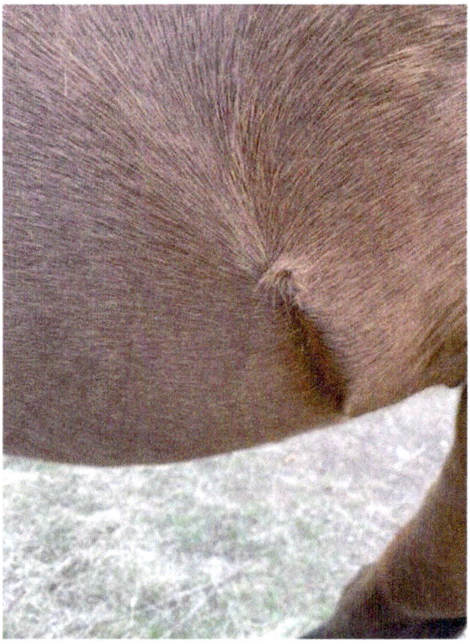

Although this horse has large belly whorls on both sides, he obviously doesn't have any weight issues. With his fit and athletic build, it is hard to see any way in which the whorls affect him.

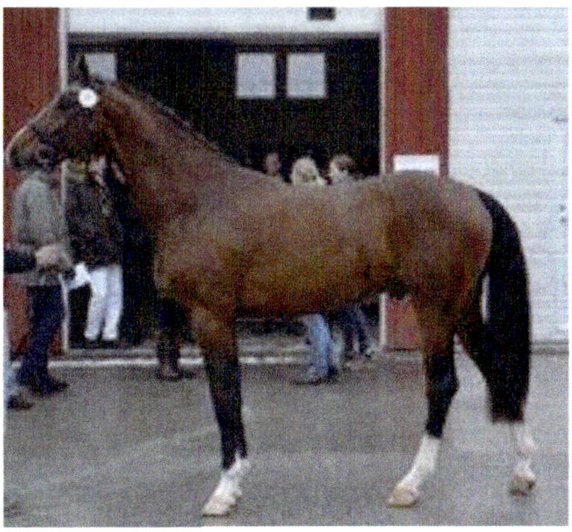

Wither Whorl

There are superstitions that a horse with a whorl on the wither is bad luck. What could cause people to think a certain whorl is bad luck? If we think about it, we can come up with many possibilities.

When saddled or in harness, a whorl on the wither is in a position that may receive lots of pressure. Pressure on a focus point like a whorl could easily cause pain and discomfort resulting in poor behavior. A horse who bucks or balks when worked would be bad luck indeed.

A horse tends to curve around a small tight whorl. This could cause a horse with a small whorl on the wither to be hollow and carry himself in an upside-down frame. A horse with a large splaying whorl would hunch up into it.

When the whorl is only on one side, horses are said to curl around it even more strongly than they normally do around unmatched whorls in other areas.

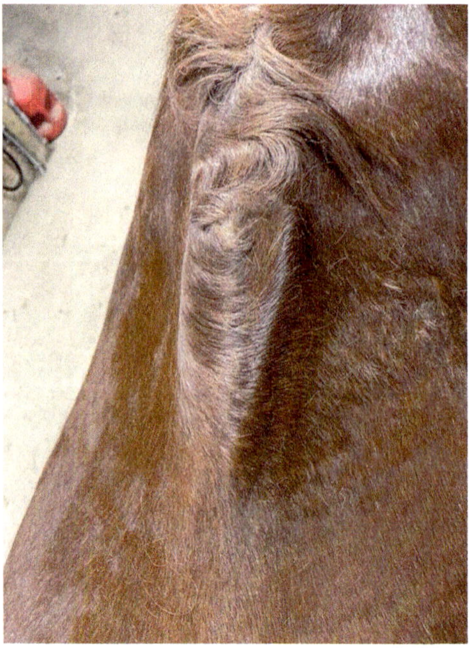

Despite the bad reputation that comes with wither whorls many horses who possess them turn out great. This horse jumps very successfully. He has a huge stride and his person says he is "a LOT of horse".

Back Whorls

Whorls on a horse's back are extremely rare, but when they do occur, it is usually between the flanks. It has been said that a whorl in this location shows a horse who will lack coordination in the hind end, be chronically sore in the back, or be otherwise lame.

There are many stories of horses with this whorl having problems. Is it because the whorl guarantees problems? Or could it be like other whorls that are said to show problem horses when it is actually a sign that rough, forceful training methods haven't been effective on these horses?

While horses with a back whorl should not be assumed to have problems, care should be taken in training to build the muscle and bring them along slowly.

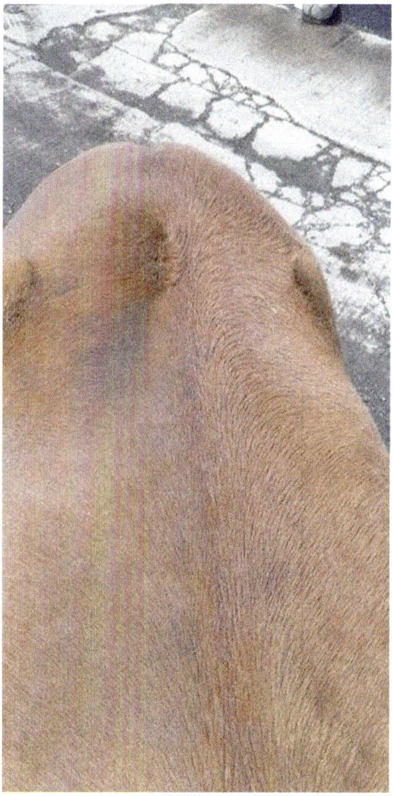

This horse is being brought along in his training slowly and carefully. This helps him to build the muscle and learn to carry himself and a rider properly and with coordination. He has been under saddle for a year of light riding with no sign of lameness and no sign of discomfort when carrying a rider.

Girth Whorls

A horse with whorls in the girth area will usually be uncomfortable when the saddle is tightened. Trouble can be avoided by tightening the cinch or girth slowly and politely.

Sometimes it is easy to see the reason behind superstitions surrounding whorls. This one is harder to guess. A girth whorl was said to have been a sign of good luck.

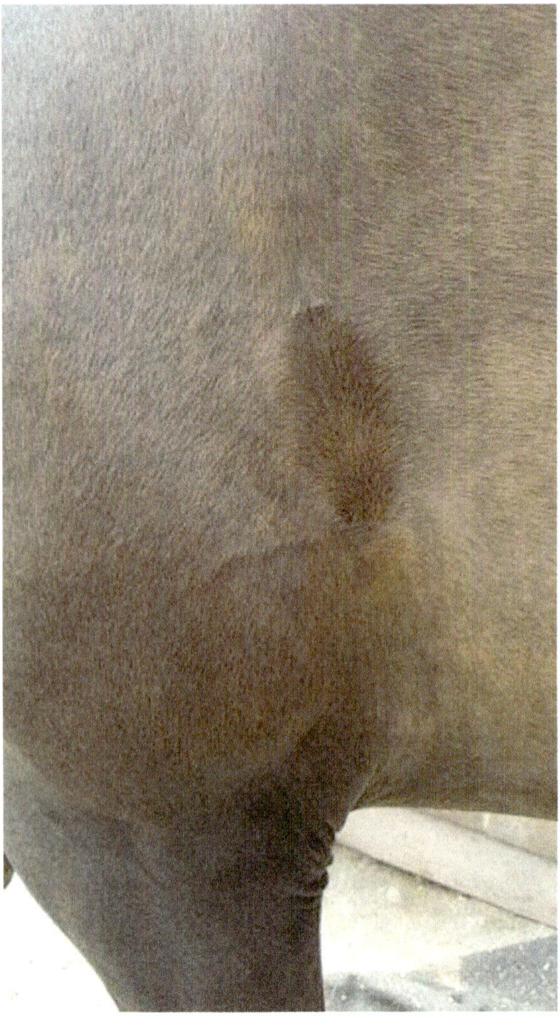

Flank Whorls

It is very important that flank whorls be matched from side to side. When flank whorls stop at different heights or begin in different places they will cause the horse to be unbalanced. This can lead to a horse who is easily spooked because their body is uncomfortable and unbalanced. Physical balance leads to emotional balance or lack thereof. When a horse is out of balance, they are more reactive when ridden and more likely to be lame.

We need to ride in a way that creates balance in a horse, and when these whorls are uneven that is nearly impossible. Horses with uneven flank whorls will bend easily one direction and have a hard time flexing to the other. Their leads will be difficult to pick up, and turns will be crooked.

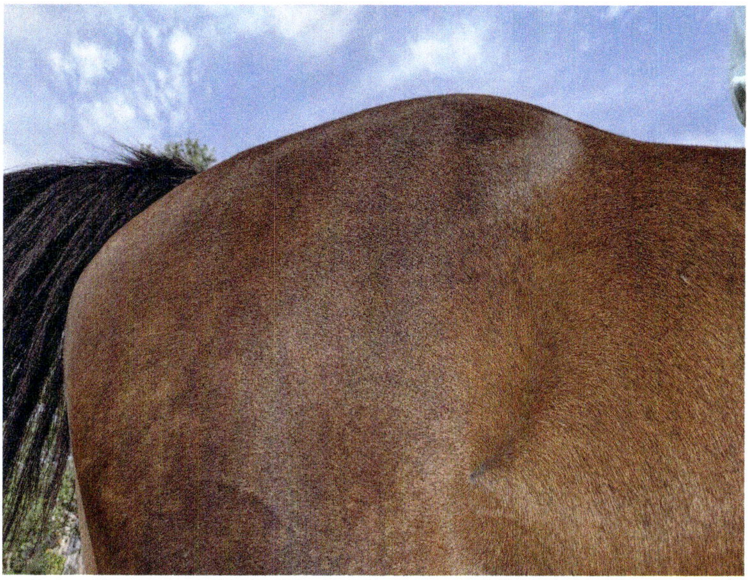

When the bottom of the whorl tips backwards towards the hind legs, the hind legs will tend to trail out behind instead of reaching underneath the body.

A break in the line of the flank whorl will cause the side with the break to be tight. The horse will curve around the side of the flank whorl with a break if it is only on one side. When the flank whorl has equal-sized breaks on both sides, it will keep the horse even and not cause problems.

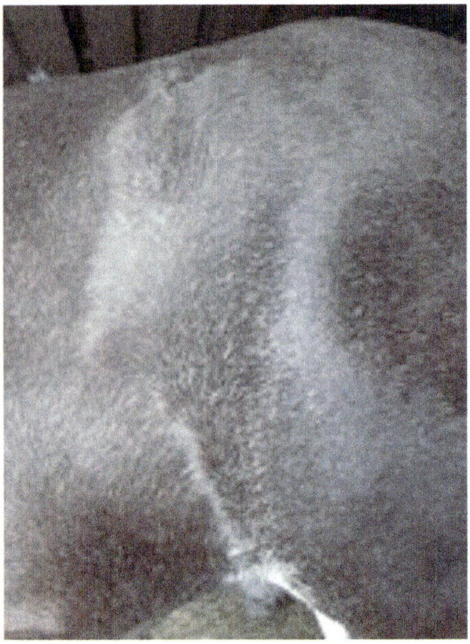

This horse's flank whorl has a branch that comes off in the middle and goes towards the belly. It is the same on both sides. He has trouble with lameness in the hind end. This sort of branching or any sort of whorl up against the side of the flank whorls seem to show lameness or unsteadiness in the hind end.

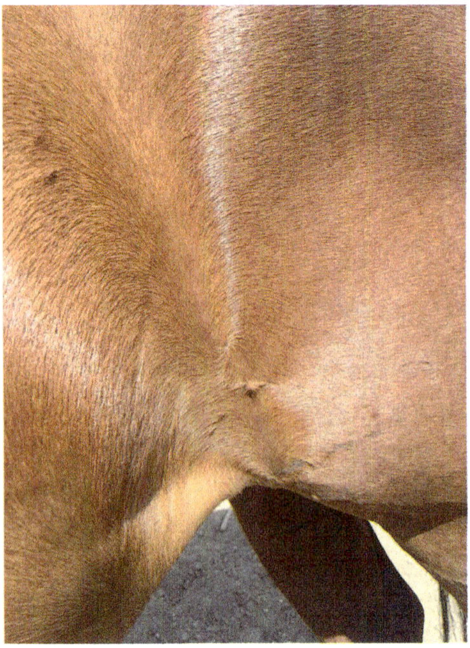

Here we see a larger whorl at the base of this flank whorl and a space before the flank whorl begins. This horse only has the break on this side. He curves tightly to the left and has trouble turning to the right. His tightness to the left is emphasized by chest whorls.

Whorls On The Hindquarters

Often we will see a line whorl up the hind leg or on the buttocks of a horse. According to lore, whorls on the hindquarters create a horse with more go than whoa. This same lore says that a horse with large whorls on the chest will have more whoa than go. Whether that's true or not remains a mystery.

Hindquarter whorls do seem to appear on horses with a lot of energy and desire to go.

A whorl on the body usually tightens the muscle where it is located. A horse will bend around a whorl that is only on one side. A whorl on the hindquarters seems to have the same effect. By tightening the muscle down the back of the leg, it prevents the leg from reaching forward under the horse. While being very energetic, horses with this whorl tend to trail their hind legs out behind.

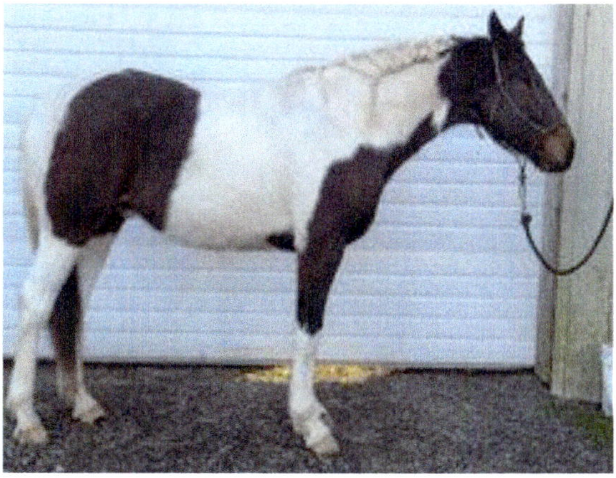

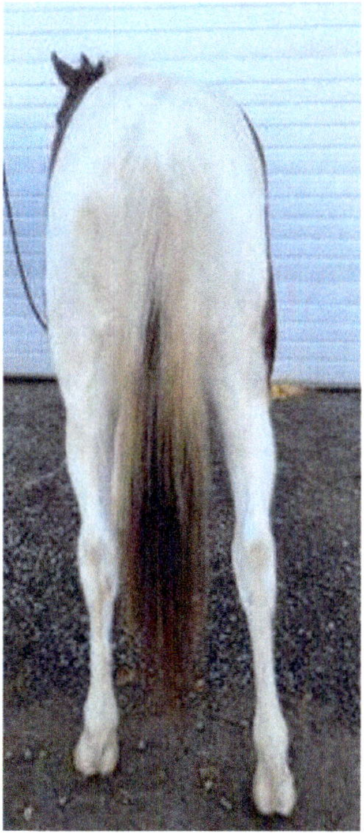

Powerful hindquarters usually accompany whorls in this area.

In cattle, a whorl up the hindquarters in the same position is said to show a cow with high butter fat content in her milk. One who will raise a good, healthy, fat calf. Does it mean the same in horses? That's hard to say. I have come across horses with these whorls who were great brood mares. Whorls keep the same meaning across species for the most part, so there's no reason to think it wouldn't show a horse who produces good, rich milk.

The most important thing is that the whorls match on both sides of the hindquarters, so the gait is even. If not, the horse will move more easily towards the side with the single whorl.

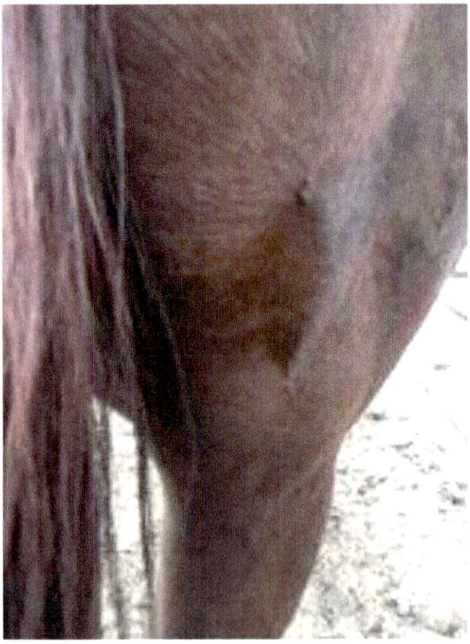

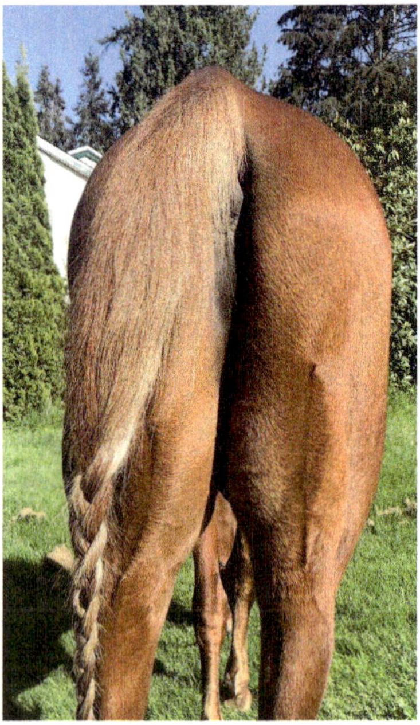

Hindquarter whorls can be straight up the back of the hindquarters or off to the side. They can also be different heights. When one whorl is higher than the other the side with the higher whorl will be the stronger side, depending on what the whorls across the rest of the body are like.

Legs Whorls

Whorls on a horse's legs are said to shorten the stride of whichever leg or legs they are found on.

When the whorls match on pairs of legs, this doesn't cause any problems. However, unmatched whorls can cause lead preferences.

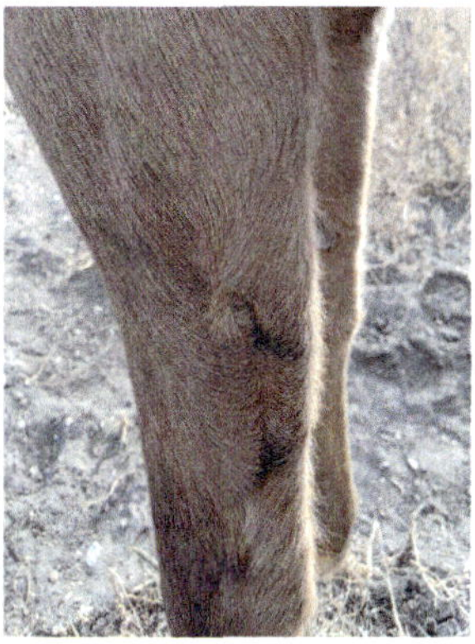

This horse prefers his left lead. There is only a whorl on his left front leg.

I have noticed that a whorl on the hind leg below the hock will often show a horse whose hind legs are crooked. Depending on the placement and size of the whorl, the horse will be anything from cow hocked to bearing a little more weight on the outside of the hoof, causing the hoof to flare towards the middle. A horse with no whorls may still be cow hocked but can tend to carry weight on the inside, with the hoof flaring outwards.

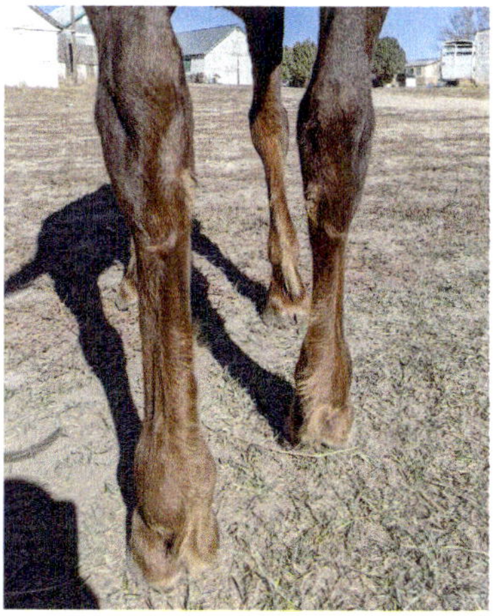

It's not only the whorls on legs that can give us information.

The size of the bone in the legs can also tell us about the animal. Studies have been done in cattle, but the overall rule applies to any animal. Larger bone generally shows a quieter animal than light bone.

By bone size, we mean the circumference of the cannon bone.

Draft horses, with their big thick legs are quieter, in general, than smaller breeds. As always, there will be exceptions.

Within a type or breed, we can also look at the size of the bone to give us a clue as to temperament. A lighter boned draft horse will be hotter than one with heavier bone. The same is true when comparing a fine boned horse of any breed with a thicker boned one. The fine-boned horse will be more high-strung.

This is something to take into consideration when looking at the entire horse. It is not something to base judgments on alone.

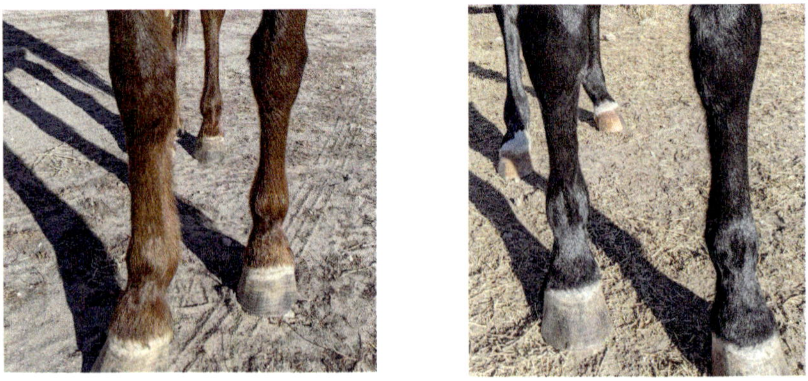

Two horses of the same breed, age, and height. Both are spirited, energetic horses, with different high whorls. The sorrel, with larger bone, measuring 8 inches, is far quieter. While the dark bay, with lighter bone, measuring 7 inches, has a stronger tendency to spook, and wants to be moving all the time.

Dropped pasterns have information to give us too.

Weak sunken pasterns can be a sign of hypermobility. Hypermobility, very briefly, is when the horse's tendons are weak and have too much stretch. When this shows in the hind legs it is often referred to as DSLD, Degenerative Suspensory Ligament Disease. This disorder, though visible in the legs, occurs through the entire body.

These weak ligaments leave horses feeling unbalanced and insecure in their movement.

That lack of control over the body causes the horse to be more reactive and likely to spook.

The importance of the way a horse feels throughout the entire body and how it affects temperament can not be overstated. We have to look at the whole horse, never just the head.

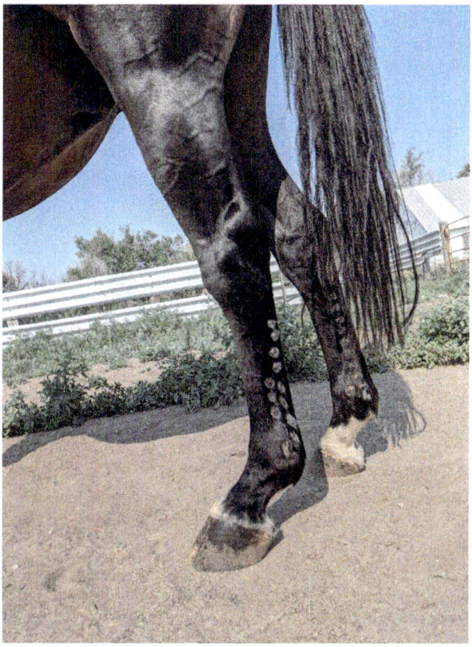

Crushed Velvet

When a horse's hair lies in many different directions, we call it crushed velvet or puzzle coat. Although the crushed velvet coat pattern is not technically a whorl, it can still give us information regarding our horses.

The exact cause is not known for sure, most likely because there are so many different causes.

One possibility is that the fascia, a web-like structure of collagen and elastin that connects and surrounds the nerves, blood vessels, organs, bones, and muscles within the horse's body, is restricted, causing the uneven lay of the hair.

Fascial tissue can become restricted and inflamed for many reasons, including injury, stress, overuse, and poor nutrition. Since fascia is a single system, the pulling caused by restriction begins to affect seemingly unrelated areas of the body, such as the hair.

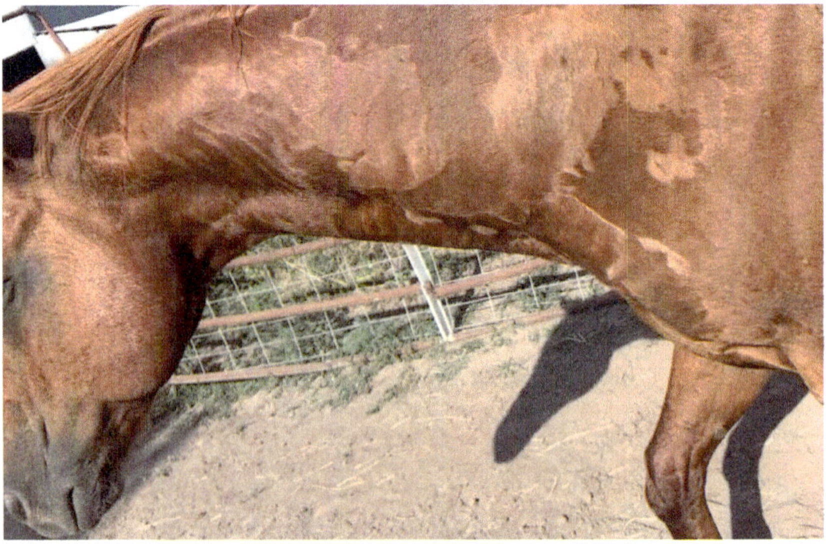

Along these same lines, horses also have arrector pili muscles. This is a band of smooth muscle that attaches to the hair follicle and the skin. It causes the hair to stand up, which helps keep horses warm by forming a layer of air between the surface of the hair and the skin. Those muscles can become inflamed, causing the hair to stand or lay differently than normal.

Massage has been shown to cause the hair to resume a normal pattern in cases where the crushed velvet coat pattern results from fascia or arrector pili muscle damage. Along with helping the hair lay flat, the massage can also help the horse to flex and softens the connective tissue.

If the crushed velvet pattern shows up only when the horse is sweating, it is a very different matter. If a horse's sweat patterns are uneven and ruffled, like the crushed velvet pattern, it can show a horse who is bracing during work or carrying himself crookedly. When a horse carries himself evenly and uses his muscles well, the hair should lay smoothly, even when the horse is sweaty.

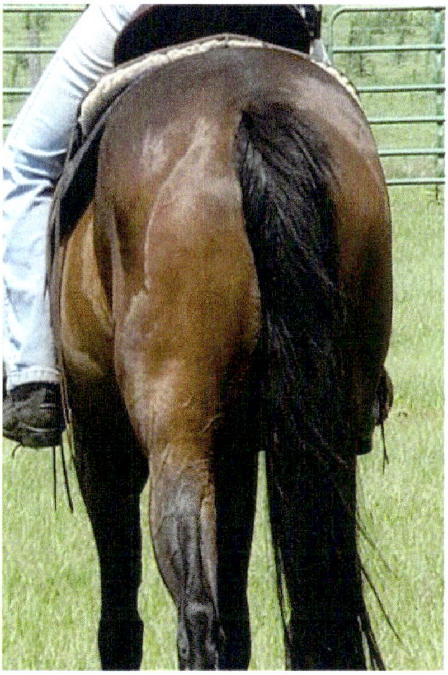

Crushed velvet occurs all over the body, not just on the neck. Sometimes it can be nothing more than a line in the hair.

An allergic reaction to bug bites or fly spray can cause a horse's hair to rise in a manner that resembles crushed velvet.

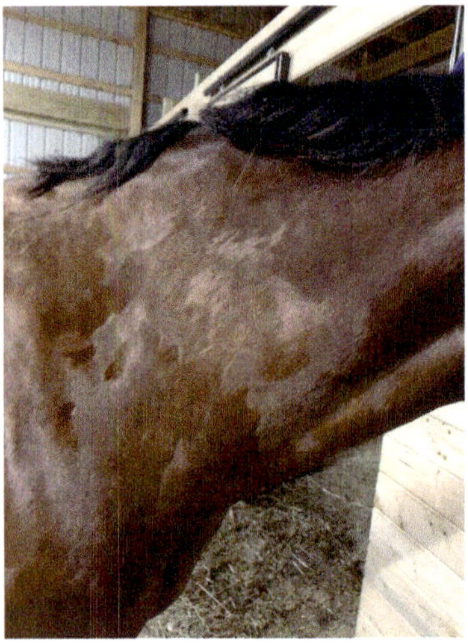

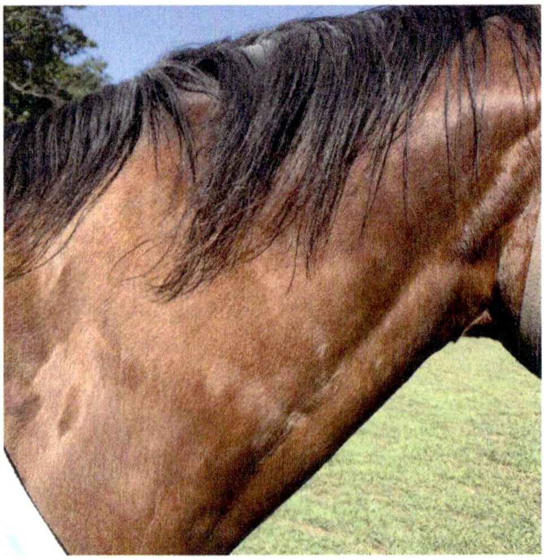

These pictures are of *the same horse when suffering from allergies, and after a solution had been found and he was comfortable again.*

When determining the cause of the crushed velvet pattern, it is important to take all factors into consideration. Has it always been there? Has there been a change in training or riding schedule? Did it occur suddenly, and are the bugs bad? Has your horse shown any signs at all of soreness?

Prophet’s Thumbprint

A Prophet's Thumbprint is a divot or dent in the muscle, usually on the side of the neck or along the hindquarters in places where the muscle is thick.

While there is an old story of this mark's origin, the true cause is much less romantic.

It is commonly believed that they are the result of a foals hoof placement in the womb. However, this isn’t proven, and many foals will not have the mark in the first few months, only to develop it later. It also doesn’t explain the appearance of the mark on the horses hindquarters, where hooves are unlikely to reach.

The marks are commonly caused by the local loss of a small amount of muscle tissue. They are usually the result of an injury, getting kicked or running into something, or possibly a hoof in the womb. Anything that causes local nerve injury can leave this mark as a long-term result because the muscle needs an intact nerve supply to function. Any injury or disease process that causes local nerve injury can also cause a small, focused area of muscle loss.

While the mark has no effect on the horse’s soundness or athletic ability, unfortunately it also has no effect on temperament or ability to predict a great horse.

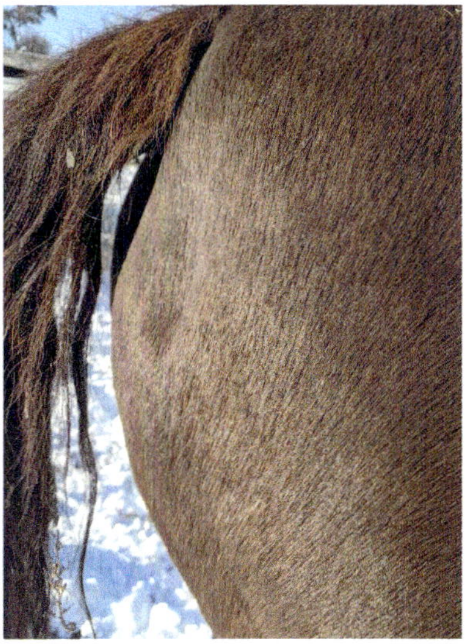

The Legend Of The Thumb Print

"The Prophet Mohammed was wandering the desert with his herd of horses for many days, and as they approached an oasis he sent them forth to drink. But as the thirsty horses approached the water, he called them back. Only five of his mares stopped and returned to him, and to thank them for their loyalty he blessed them by pressing his thumbprint into their necks. It's believed that a horse with such a mark will be outstanding, being a descendant of one of these brood mares that the Prophet Mohammed particularly treasured."

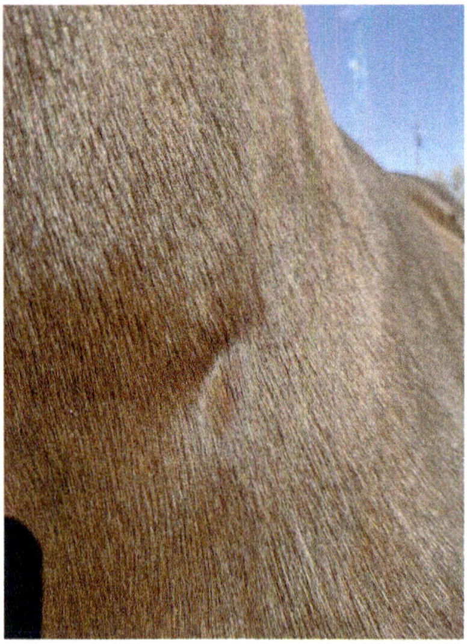

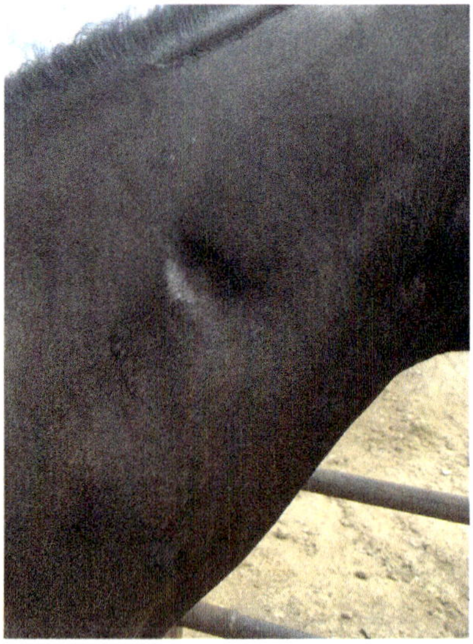

The prophets thumbprint on two different necks in two different locations. They can be anywhere on the body and vary from deep to only a slight imprint.

Head Shape

While we can tell a lot about a horse by their whorls, we can tell so much more when we combine those whorls with the shape of the head. A horse who has a high whorl and a dished profile will be completely different than a horse with a high whorl and a convex profile. Both horses will be extroverts, but the one with the dish will be right-brained while the convex profile will likely be left-brained. When trying to judge temperament, it is very useful to have the full story and not just pieces of it.

Straight

The profile of an average horse is almost perfectly straight. Sometimes this will have the effect of making the head look like a rectangle from the side. This shows a horse who is quiet and dependable, depending on what the rest of the head says about him.

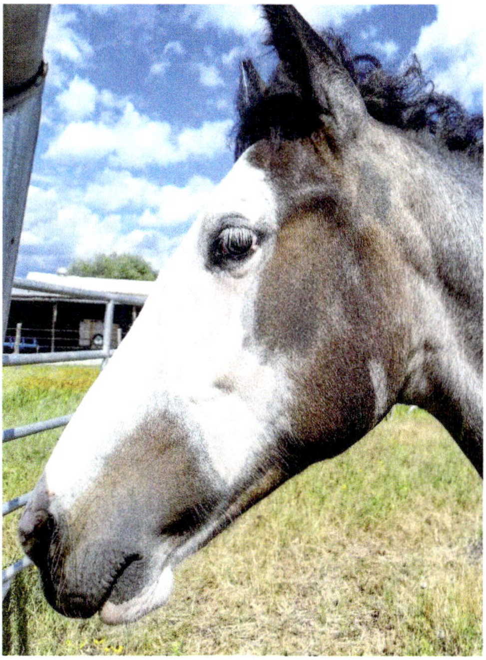

Convex

A horse whose profile and nose curves outwards is usually a tough character, bold and confident. The placement and extremity of the outward curve can make a big difference in the exact temperament.

When the curve is only above the nose, it is a moose nose and shows intelligence and confidence.

When the curve is more of a Roman nose, starting below the eyes and rounding down to the muzzle, the horse is physically tough and sometimes said to be stubborn.

When the entire head is rounded, from above the eyes down to the nose, the horse may not be as quick to learn as a horse whose profile starts to round down lower.

A horse with a strong nose bone, the bone standing out clearly from the rest of the head, will have strong opinions and want to do things their own way.

Horses with convex profiles are almost always left-brained, tough, and determined.

Concave

A concave profile is what we think of when we picture an Arabian with their classically dished head. However, the shape doesn't have to be extreme to count as concave. The slightest dip between eyes and nose counts.

As with convex profiles, there are variations to the extent of the dish.

Occasionally, a concave profile can be combined with a bulge over the forehead. This is sometimes called a jibah, and can be a sign of an extremely temperamental horse-one who is very emotional, sensitive, reactive, and often hot.

Horses with concave profiles are almost always right-brained.

Concave With A Moose Nose

There are times we can see a combination of convex and concave head shapes in a horse who has a dished face and a rounded bump over the nose. This bump is referred to as a moose nose. These horses are sensitive but also bold, confident, and extremely smart.

This horse has a pronounced moose nose and a small complex muzzle. Combined with a large jowl and large but hooded eyes, this produces a head that shows us a horse who is very smart and confident. He will be quite the character and will not take it well if his intelligence is not acknowledged.

Nostrils

If we sit and look closely at our horse's head, we begin to notice things that may have escaped our attention otherwise. Things like features on different sides of their heads being different sizes!

Even this can tell us about the horse.

For example, if a horse's nostrils are different sizes, it can show tightness or tension on the side of the body with the smaller feature.

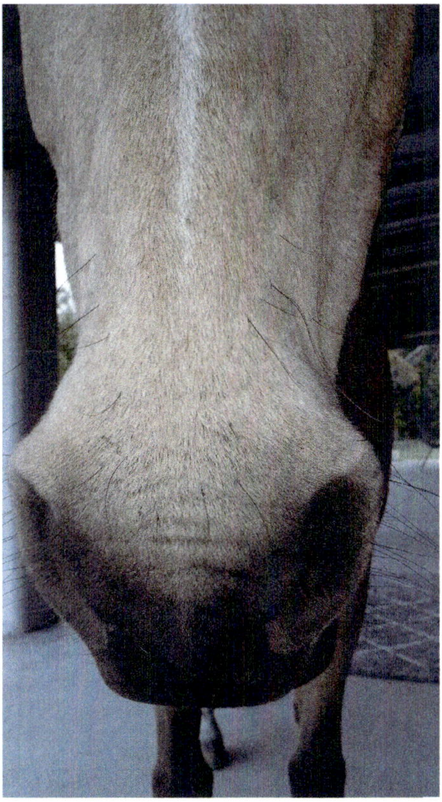

This horse has a large scar on her left shoulder that interferes with her neck and shoulder muscles. Her left nostril is smaller than her right nostril due to the tightness she carries throughout her left side. This is due to the injury but also overall stiffness.

We can tell other things by looking at the nostrils, aside from noticing if their sizes match.

Large open nostrils show intelligence and athleticism. They can be a sign that a horse is alert and aware of their surroundings. Depending on what the rest of the head looks like they can show a horse who tends to be spooky.

Small tight nostrils mark a horse who will take longer to learn new things and may not be as athletic.

Wrinkles around the nostrils show pain or disgust.

Large open nostrils show that this horse is intelligent and aware of everything around her.

Lips

One clue to a horse's personality that is never wrong is the shape of their upper lip.

A horse who isn't as interested and doesn't want to interact with everything will have a flat upper lip. This is a result of the muscles being underdeveloped through a lack of use.

Horses who are curious, interested in their surroundings, and who like to explore their world with their mouth have a pointed, shapely upper lip.

Whether the tendency to be curious comes from having a lip with this shape or if the muscles become strong and assume this shape because they get worked so often is hard to say.

Horses with this type of nose will often have a whorl right in the center of their upper lip.

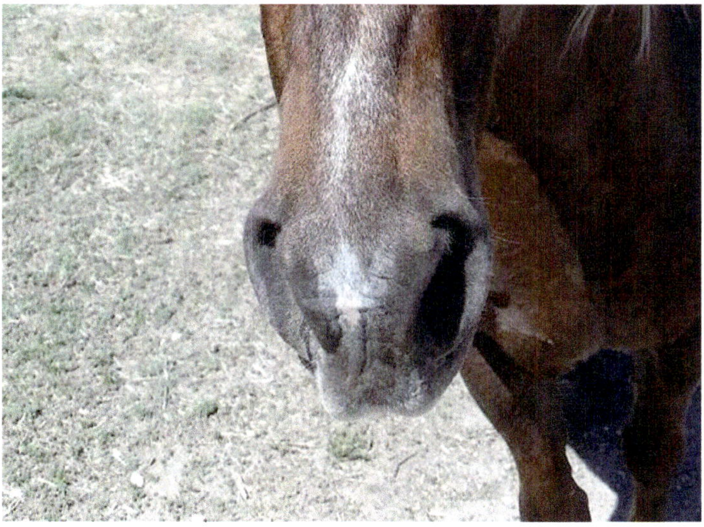

This horse will want to explore the world using his mouth. He will be curious and interested in everything around him.

Chin

A chin that is smooth and large without extra wrinkles, extreme pointedness, or overly flat is basic. It shows an average horse who is mostly steady and dependable.

When the chin has pronounced ridges, tiered like an upside-down wedding cake, it shows a horse with a complex personality. This horse will have opinions, quirks, and a mind of his own.

A very flat chin is a sign of intelligence. When the mouth ends very close to the chin, it is another sign that the horse is extremely smart. Intelligence is good unless the horse is smarter than the people trying to work with him. They can outsmart their owners.

Here we see a complex chin combined with the sloped muzzle. This horse will have strong opinions and a mind of his own.

This horse has a small pointed chin that will get rock hard when the horse is upset

Some horses will have a small pointed chin. When they get upset, the pointed part of the chin will get rock hard. When tightening their chin, the horse's lower lip splays out like that of a small child pouting. Often the muscles around the eyes will tighten too, forming wrinkles below the eye and even pulling the lower eyelid away from the eye.

While the horse might not blow up when they reach this state, it is a good sign to let us know we need to step back and help the horse calm down and make whatever we were attempting easier through smaller steps and less pushing. Nothing can be accomplished until their chin relaxes back to normal.

Ears

We hear a lot of lore about the meaning of horses' whorls, head shapes, and color from old wives' tales and legends. While a lot of it can easily be dismissed, there are some legends that carry truth with them.

One is that curvy ears show a hot horse. It is well agreed upon that hotter horses will have more shapely and curvaceous ears. In contrast, quieter horses will have broad ears with little definition. Ears that go straight up or get closer together at the tips show hotter horses, while ears that spread apart towards the tips show a calmer horse.

When a horse regularly carries their ears pricked forward, we can tell they are an extrovert. A horse who has a tendency to carry their ears back will be an introvert. This is not related to when a horse is mad and pins their ear back as a warning. Some horses have a habit of going about with their ears laid slightly back. It isn't a threat, just the way they carry themselves.

This horse has hot, forward picked ears, small and curvy. They show a horse who is energetic, forward, and emotional.

When the ears lay out to the sides, they are known as Lop ears. These are a sign of an extremely quiet, easy-going horse.

Generally, the wider the ears are spaced the quieter the horse is. Horses with ears that are set wide on the head and spread even wider at the tips will be willing and steady.

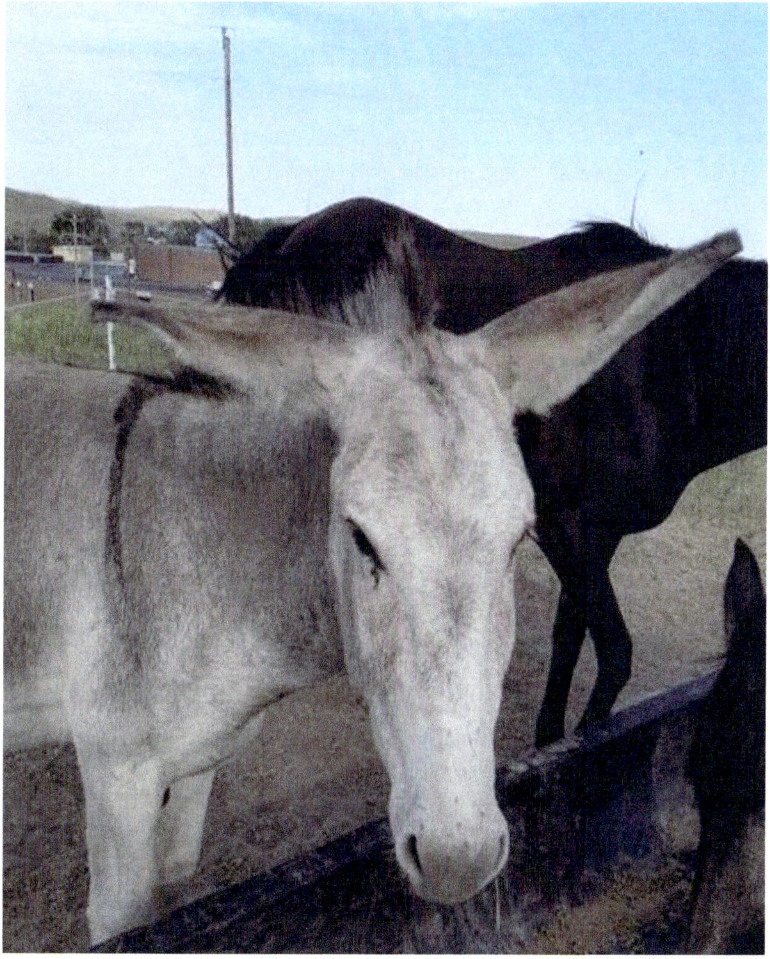

Along with lop ears showing an exceptionally quiet friendly nature, this donkey shows the low whorl that is typical for donkeys and mules.

This horse has wide-set ears that are also very wide themselves. Both traits show calm steadiness. The sharp point they come to adds a dash of sensitivity and intelligence.

Superstition has it that horses with long ears make the best jumpers. Mules are usually spectacular jumpers who can clear jumps taller than they are from a standstill, so maybe there's some truth to that legend.

A horse with long skinny ears, can be changable and temperamental. These are set wider at the tips than the base, so that may add some dependability and steadiness.

Jowls

Large jowls show a horse that is athletic and a quick learner. Likely, they seem smarter because they can take in large amounts of air, allowing them to perform and learn easier. Large jowls don't mean a horse will be agile or nimble, just that they will be athletic in their ability to not get winded.

Smaller jowls can be a sign of a horse that doesn't learn as easily. That doesn't mean they can't learn, just that more time might be needed to teach a lesson. Horses who don't learn as quickly can be suitable for beginning riders who may otherwise teach a horse bad habits.

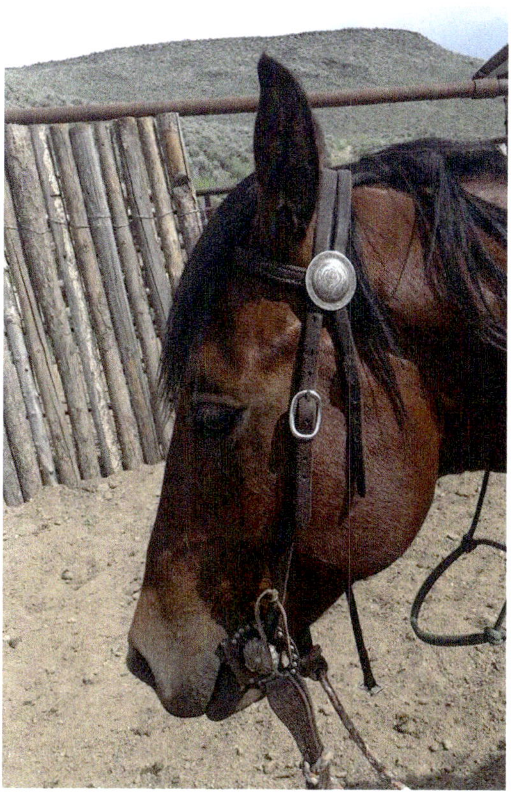

Large athletic jowls, combined with a very straight profile and squared-off muzzle show a horse who is athletic, smart, steady, and willing.

Eyes

It is said that the eyes are the windows to the soul. I guess that could be true, we can learn a lot about a horse from their eyes.

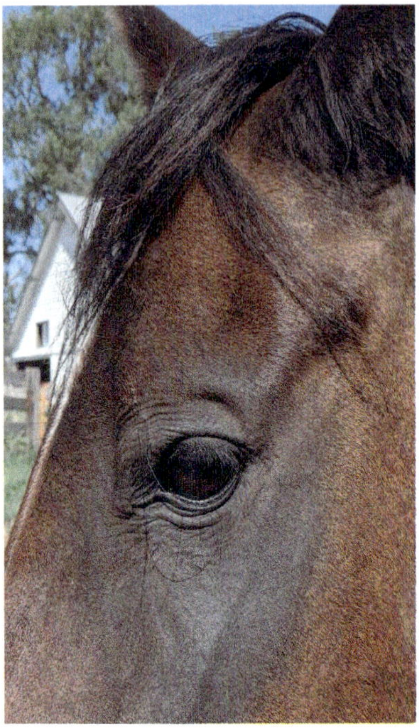

Lines and wrinkles around the eye can be a sign of stress or pain. Although some horses, when enjoying a good scratch, can wrinkle the skin around their eyes until the pink inside the lid shows. Those same wrinkles under different circumstances could be a sign of discomfort. It is always important to take all aspects of a horse and its environment into account when making judgments.

A small eye, or pig eye, shows a horse who will learn a little slower. This can be beneficial because they won't learn bad habits easily. Once they know their job, they will do it without over thinking and causing trouble. Patience and taking the time to let them figure out what is being asked of them will avoid a fight and produce a steady, willing horse.

Large eyes show intelligence. Among large eyes, there are different types. Some eyes are big, soft, and kind. These horses are trusting. They look to people for support and reassurance.

Other eyes are hard and distant, the look of eagles. These horses are very smart, capable, and a bit standoffish.

This horse has a large, kind eye combined with a slight moose nose and large jowl.

When the forehead between the eyes is very wide, it is a sign of a quick learner. This can be a drawback for a beginner just learning themselves. But is great for an experienced trainer who can keep up.

A horse with very narrow forehead may take a little longer to grasp new concepts. Slow, careful tutoring keeps them from getting frustrated. Once they've learned a lesson, they are less likely to come up with their own variations unlike a horse with a wider forehead.

A broad forehead and widely spaced ears. Eyes are clearly visible from the front, as are the large jowls and inquisitive upper lip.

Eyes should be set so we can see them when looking at the horse from the front. If we can't see their eyes, they can't see us.

When horses' eyes are set too far to the sides of the head, they can have trouble seeing in front of them and may spook when things suddenly pop into view.

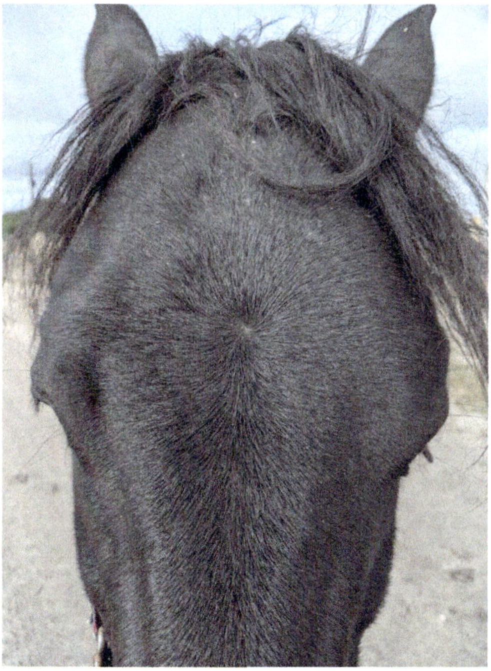

Superstition has it that horses with white around their eyes are crazy.

When a horse doesn't usually have white that shows, white rims can be a sign that the horse is upset.

Many horses naturally have white around the eyes, and it is only the coloring, not a sign of temperament.

Brain Muscle

Often horses will have ridges on each side of their forehead, above each eye. Sometimes they are large and very noticeable; other times, they are practically nonexistent. These are lovingly referred to as brain muscle, or in some areas, brain lines.

In reality, these are the temporalis muscles. They are responsible for opening and closing the jaw.

While it is possible they may not actually be a sign of a strong mind, they can tell us a lot about the horse. If the muscles are larger on one side than the other, it is a sign of dental problems. Dental issues in horses can cause pain and headaches, just like they do in humans.

Pain is a very common source of behavioral issues. If we think there may be some imbalance in the temporalis muscle, we can check by gently probing the area.

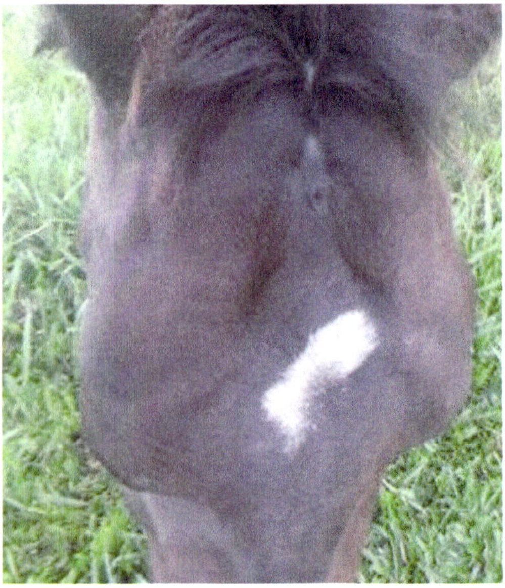

A horse who is sore will show the usual reactions to pain, trying to pull their head away and flinching from the pressure.

These muscles may not be able to tell us if our horses are smart or not, but they can be clues as to our horses' dental health.

Horns

Alright, maybe these structures are not really 'horns'. However some horses will have bumps protruding from the head above their eyes. These are actual bony growths on the skull. Although they are usually located on the forehead, the horns can occur anywhere in the poll area.

Alexander the Great's horse Bucephalus (which means ox head) was known for having horns. There are a few breeds of horse known for having horns, the Moyle horse developed in Utah, the Carthusian strain of Andalusians, and the ancient Datong breed of horse from China. Horns are now considered to be a flaw in Datong horses and are not bred for. The horns can occur on other horse breeds too. Apparently, a recessive trait that can pop up, seemingly out of nowhere.

This is not a common feature, we seldom see horses adorned with horns. The ones we do see seem to share a few common features. Their owners say they may not be the brightest horses. Dopey, slow, and not overly bright are common descriptions.

They also describe their horses as very friendly, easy-going, and willing, to the best of their capabilities.

It is entirely possible that there are temperament traits that accompany these growths. The breeds known for having horns are also known for extraordinary endurance and extreme docility.

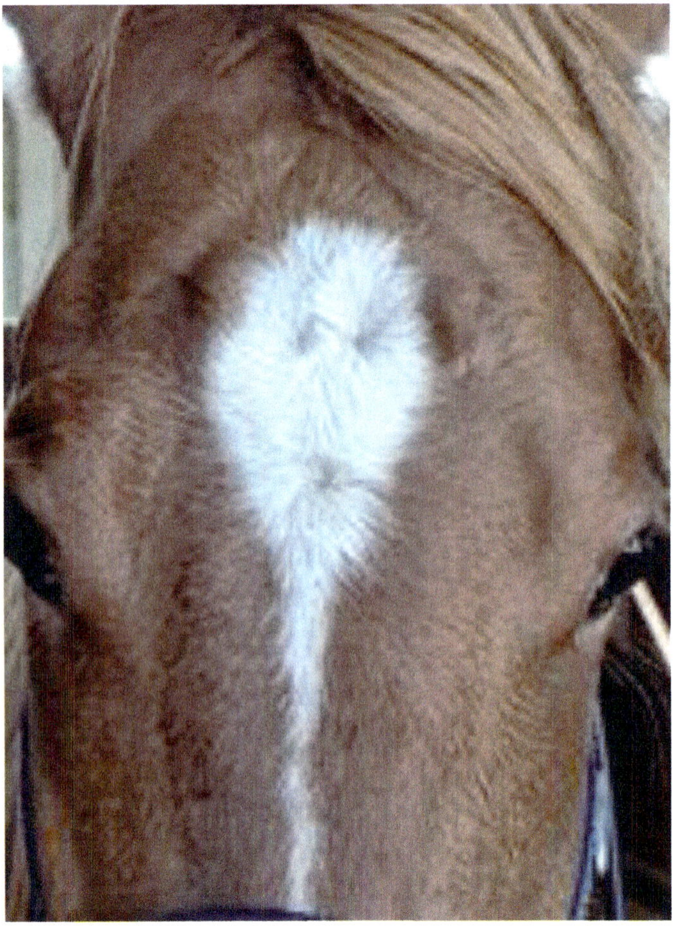

Pain Faces, Horse Grimace Scale

Horses only have 17 separate facial actions that they are capable of alternating between when showing emotion. Compared to the 27 facial actions in humans, that may not be a lot, but it's enough to give us a good idea about what is going on inside our horses by looking at their expressions.

Horses move their facial muscles in much the same way humans do, using their mouth, lips, chin, and eyes to convey emotion. We use our faces to show emotion similarly enough that horses are able to read human facial expression. Studies have shown that horses prefer to go to a person who is smiling and will avoid people who frown. Horses will go so far as to remember the last facial expression they saw on the person and avoid people who frowned the last time they saw them, even when that was days before.

Tightness around the nose and mouth can be a sign of pain. So can head carriage, wrinkles around the eyes, and ears held stiffly back

Horses raise their inner eyebrows to show concern or fear. They can wrinkle their nostrils in disgust or dislike. Many horses can flatten or tighten their chin when upset.

They grimace in pain, so well in fact, that there is a Horse Grimace Scale to help veterinarians determine when a horse is suffering.

On this scale, pain is determined by how much a horse is showing each related behavior, in regards to:

- Orbital tightening
- Tension above the eye area
- Strained chewing muscles
- Strained mouth and pronounced chin
- Stiffly backward ears
- Strained nostrils and flattening of the profile

Close attention to clues like these given by our horses can help us to recognize when our horses are in pain, even when the cause of that pain is not clearly visible.

Colors

Most superstitions about telling a horse's temperament by their color are merely that, superstition. High white socks don't show a horse who is crazy, and white hooves are just as strong as dark hooves. Bruising is just easier to see on a light color. Red mares aren't really evil, although according to Klause Hempfling, classical horsemen considered chestnuts not suitable for riding. They were thought to be headstrong and have heart and circulatory problems, as well as suffering from eye issues. Having ridden and loved many healthy chestnut horses, I can't say I've seen anything to support that.

That said, there are some things color can tell us...

Horses carrying the silver dapple gene also carry the eye issues that come with it. Including the bulbous bulging of the eye, iridal hypoplasia, uveal cysts, cataracts, and even retinal detachment.

White near the ears of a horse can be a sign of problems. Although deafness is rare in horses, when white markings extend up the forehead to the ears, it can cause a congenital form of "splashed-white" deafness. This is caused by the alteration of the receptor cells in the horse's inner ear.

Noticed to be deaf in his mid-twenties this horse was likely deaf his whole life. White doesn't have to be excessive to lead to deafness, and not all horses with large white markings will be deaf.

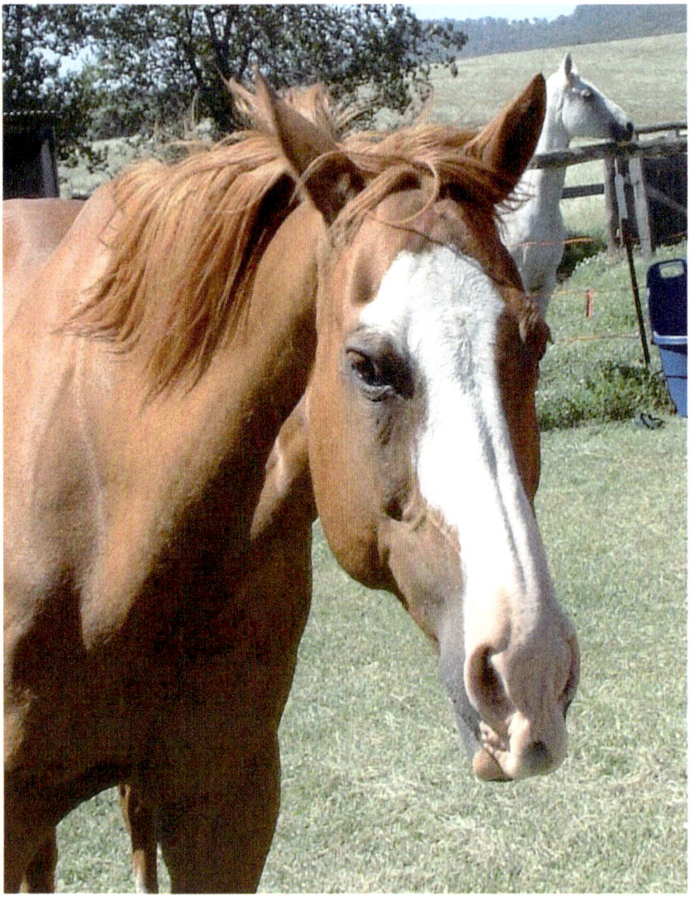

Grey horses need a whole section of their own. They tend to have shorter lives, at least partially due to the prevalence of melanoma. As many as eighty percent of grey horses over the age of fifteen have some form of melanoma.

The color grey is actually a pigment disease that causes melanocytes to overproduce pigment, and then burn out. The flea 'bites' on a flea-bitten grey are where melanocytes "reignite" in late stages of greying, causing dark spots to appear. The color of the flea bites are not related to the base color of the horse. They occur more commonly on heterozygous greys, that is, horses who carry only one copy of the grey gene.

Although it isn't a whorl, anything on the outside of a horse that gives us clues as to what is going on inside the horse is of interest. The story of the Bloody Shoulder, often found on Arabians, is too much fun to skip.

A powerful sheik was injured in battle. His trusty mare carried him home as he lay helpless across her back. He was dead when they arrived. His mare gave birth shortly after to a foal marked with the same pattern of blood on his shoulder as the mare had been marked with by her master's blood. The mark was passed on as a sign that any horse who carries it will possess remarkable loyalty and bravery.

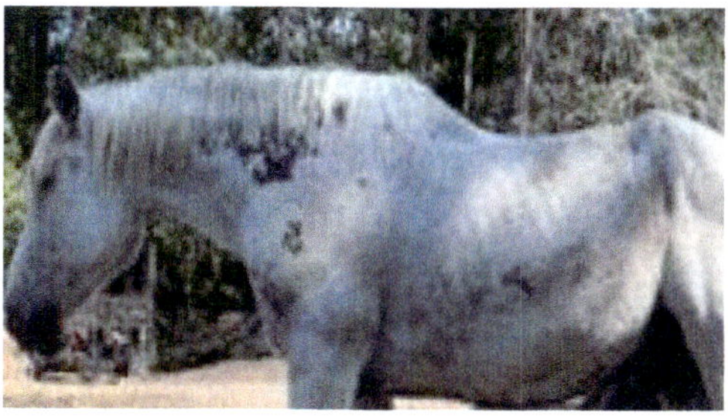

The coloring is actually a collection of densely packed fleabites and can show up anywhere on the body, in any breed. The story makes it more fun though.

Whorls On Donkeys

Donkeys are almost like horses, but not quite. It is fitting then that their whorls are judged almost the same as horses, but not quite. Mules, also almost like horses but not quite, can be judged much the same as donkeys.

Even though a donkey has a much wider forehead than horses, the donkey's olfactory bulbs are much smaller and rotate inward. Horses have large olfactory bulbs located in the front of the brain, and normal, basic horse whorls are usually within one and a half centimeters of them.

In donkeys, the whorls are located far from the olfactory bulbs. Their whorls are much farther down the head, almost always below eye level.

This is significant because of the role scent plays in a horse's life, in social interactions, memory, and learning. Scent is like a language to horses, and donkeys. The fact that whorls are placed in such careful relation to them backs up whorl theory even more.

That donkey and mule whorls don't line up with the olfactory lobes doesn't debunk the theory, instead it gives us a different set of rules.

This donkey has double stacked whorls. She is emotional, shy, easily scared, but also gentle and sweet.

To judge the whorls on donkeys and mules, we take the same locations we use when looking at horses' heads and move them down.

A whorl between the eyes is high for a donkey. Mid nose is a center whorl. Whorls nearly to the muzzle are low whorls that would show an introvert. Not having whorls above the eyes doesn't mean that there aren't extrovert donkeys.

No whorls at all are far more common with donkeys than they are in horses.

Head shape can be judged in donkeys and mules too. Dished still shows a sensitive animal, and convex shows a tough and determined one. They have different basic shapes, but as long as we compare donkeys to donkeys and not to horses, we can get a good idea of temperament.

All donkeys have a cross on their back, going down the top line like dorsal stripes on a dun, then across their shoulders and down the sides. Sometimes, as a donkey ages, the marking will fade, but it is still there to be seen on the skin if you shave the coat.

Like with the Prophets Thumbprint, the Donkey's Cross has its own story.

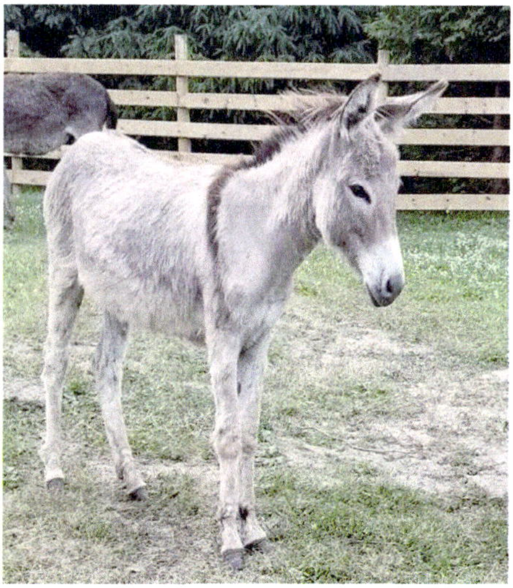

The Donkey's Cross

Jesus chose a humble animal, the donkey, to ride into the city of Jerusalem. In the ancient Middle Eastern world, leaders rode horses if they rode to war, but donkeys if they came in peace. Rather than riding to conquer, this king would enter in peace.

Jesus counted the donkey as equal to every other living being and rode the donkey to show His humility because donkeys are plain, humble creatures. There is nothing fancy or glorious about them. But they are good servants to humans. They do their job without vanity or ego.

As they approached Jerusalem and came to Bethphage on the Mount Of Olives, Jesus sent two disciples, saying to them, "Go to the village ahead of you, and at once you will find a donkey tied there, with her colt by her. Untie them and bring them to Me. If anyone says anything to you, tell him that The Lord needs them, and he will send them right away."

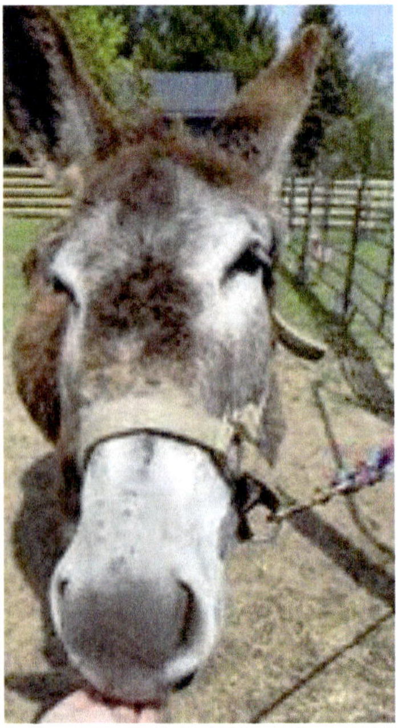

They brought the donkey and the colt, placed their cloaks on the donkey, and Jesus sat on her.

Because the humble little donkey carried Jesus as He went to be crucified, the donkey was marked with the sign of the cross to show others His love and devotion.

Whorls In Cattle

Extensive studies have been done on whorls in cattle and their effect on temperament. In many ways cattle are easier to study than horses. They aren't usually handled as much as horses, so there isn't as much influence from nurture, we mostly get to see what was given by nature. Entire herds of cattle are routinely handled in exactly the same manner. Such as when they are run through a chute to be given shots. This allows us to judge large groups who have all received the same 'training'.

Cattle with high whorls have been found to be far more reactive in the chute. In horses, a high whorl shows an extrovert who is energetic and reactive. It makes sense that the whorls would mean the same things in cattle. The only question with cattle is, what does an extroverted cow look like? What does an introverted cow look like?

An interesting look at the heredity of whorls. A Hereford cow and two of her white-faced heifers. This year's calf with no whorls, just like mom, while the calf from two years ago has a single center whorl.

One person, whose steer had three whorls low on his face, said her steer was "so calm if he didn't blink you'd be checking for a pulse". Many people select their show cattle or replacement heifers based on whorls. They look for even centered whorls because those cattle can be easier to halter train and handle. They also tend to be quieter when run through a chute for routine care.

After reading the work done by Temple Grandin, my friend Cherrie was doing a college research project. Being up in front of the chute drawing blood and dosing the cattle, she was in the perfect position to take note of the whorls as over four hundred head of cattle were run through daily for two weeks. Unfortunately whorls weren't part of the study, so we don't have exact numbers. However, she did make note of them though as they went through, over and over, throughout the study.

She saw that the temperaments matched the findings in Temple Grandin's studies and that "The ones with high whorls never got accustomed to the chute, the middle whorls accepted and worked well, and the low whorls were the ones who didn't herd well or tried to find ways out of participating with the main herd."

A high whorl combined with the moderate head type, neither fully beef nor dairy, on a yearling who tends to fight in the chute. She is very curious and interested in what is going on around her when not confined.

There are benefits to high whorls on cattle. In one study, on a small number of Holstein heifers, they found that the ones with a high whorl gained weight faster than those with middle or low whorls.

Cattle who have no whorls at all on their foreheads have been found to be more likely to lose their calves to predators. Cattle with high whorls are more aware of their surroundings and will be on the look out for predators. They are the least likely to lose calves to predation. However, in a separate study, cattle with no whorl were found to be just as temperamental as the cattle with the high whorls.

As in all other species, abnormal whorls can be signs of abnormalities in cattle too. Bulls with whorls that form a long line between the eyes have lower-quality sperm than bulls with a single centrally located whorl.

An abnormal whorl can show low fertility. Any whorl that is long, a line whorl, or set off to the side, is counted as abnormal. This cow's whorl sits far off to our left.

Cattle with no whorl were found to be high-strung in one study. This cow took off the last time she was worked. She went through many fences, then turned and fought the people trying to convince her to rejoin the herd. She has a beef-type head combined with no whorl. If we look closely, we can see her eyes are cloudy and blue, this is a sign of eye problems. It is very important to take in every aspect of the animal we are looking at, not just whorls. Not being able to see clearly probably exacerbated her already high-strung temperament.

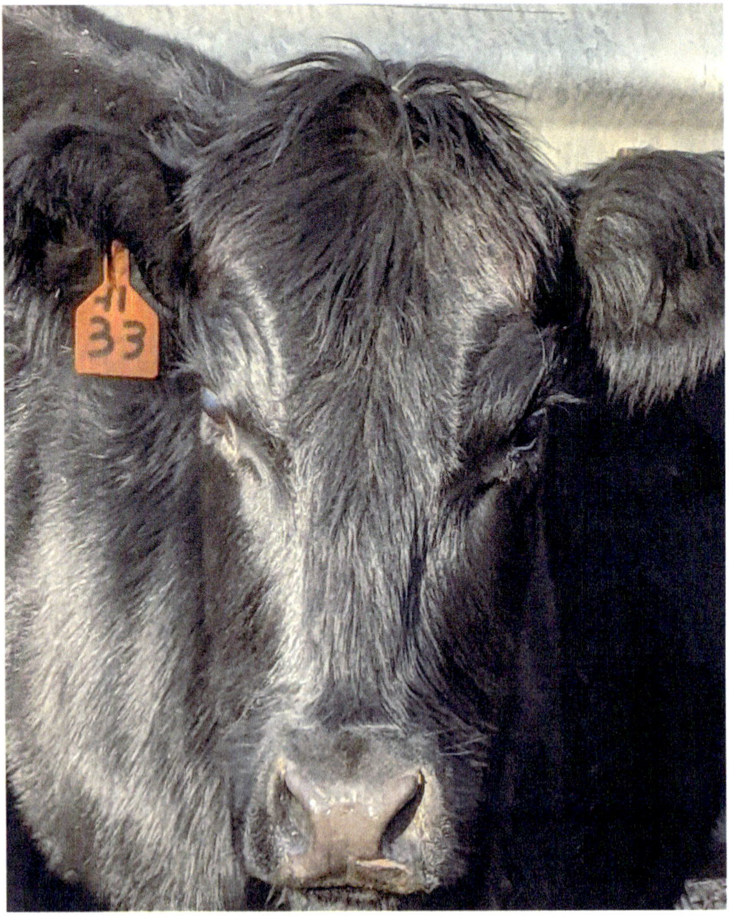

The head shape of cattle probably tells us as much as the head shape of horses. Although this has not been studied, some stories and traditions have been passed down regarding this that we can learn from.

Old cowhands said that you could tell the mean cows by their very rectangular head shape. This is not to be confused with the long narrow head shape more common to dairy cattle and some beef cattle, which shows a quieter cow. The wide short heads, more often found in beef cattle, are not as quiet or friendly. Again this head type can also be found in dairy cattle, but is less common.

It does make sense that the typical dairy cow is quieter than a beef cow. Beef cattle are carefully selected for mothering instinct, the ability to fight off predators and defend their calves. Dairy cattle are bred for ease of handling and to have little to no mothering instinct.

Unfortunately, there haven't been any studies done to uphold these theories, it would be an interesting area to look into!

A high center whorl combined with a beef type head.

The beef-type head, a more triangular shape, pronounced eyebrows, with eyes set farther apart.

A dairy-type head, longer and more narrow, eyes set deeper within the head.

Whorls on cattle that don't tell us about temperament are usually used to tell us about milk quality or fertility. Whorls on the back of the hindquarters show a cow with rich milk high in butter fat, as does an adrenal whorl that sits at or ahead of the shoulders.

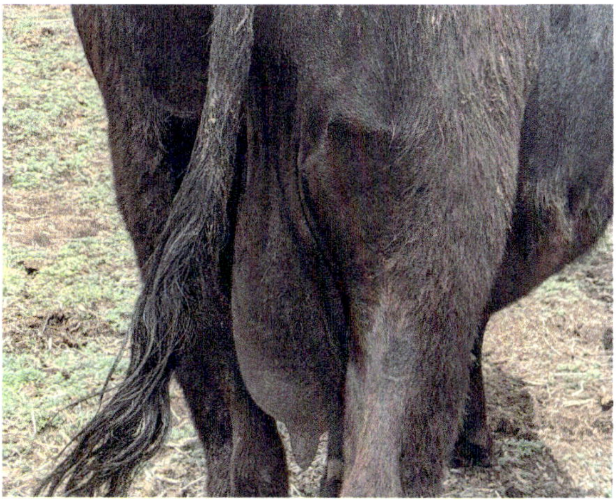

Whorls aren't the only thing cattle can be judged by; there are other indicators such as conformation and shape of certain body parts. A fertile cow is built downhill with her hind end at the flank much thicker than she is through the girth. Wrinkles in the skin show a cow who will have richer milk and more tender meat. Loose skin is a sign of a healthy fertile animal.

When looking at cattle, you can judge an approximate age by looking at their noses. Narrow noses show younger cattle. As the cow ages, the nose gets wider. Ages can be judged more exactly by looking at the teeth. An old cow is called broken mouthed because they will have teeth missing. When that isn't possible, you can get an idea of their age by their nose.

Here are one, two, and three-year-old cattle, their noses are narrow and small. There aren't yet large differences in width.

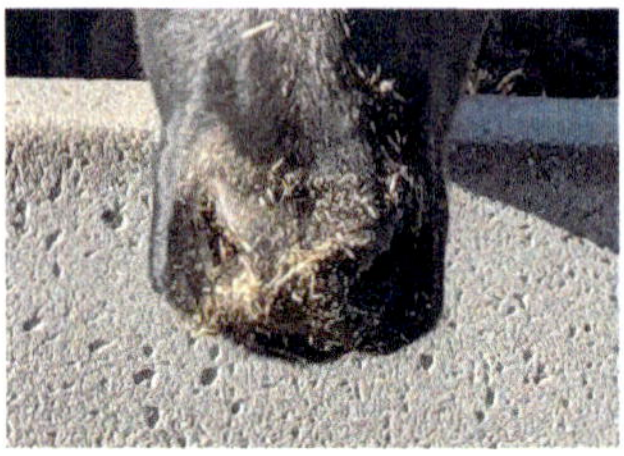

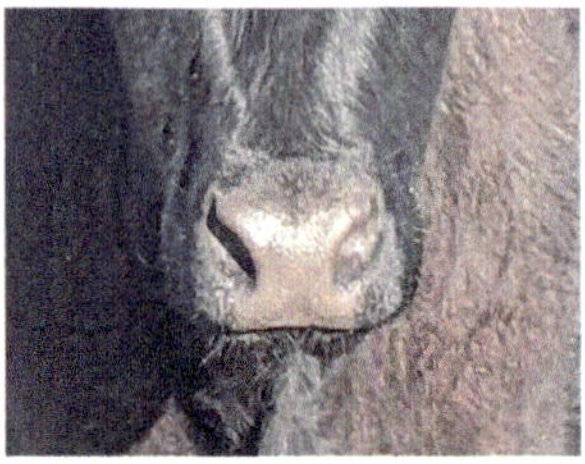

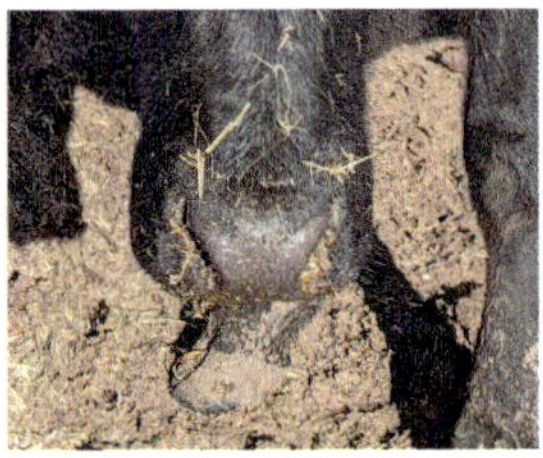

A six-year-old cow, her nose and the mouth around it are growing broader.

A well-aged cow, over ten years old. Her nose is wide, changing the shape of her head from triangular to rectangular.

Whorls In Dogs

It shouldn't come as any surprise that dogs have whorls too. A dog tends to have symmetrical whorls that initiate the direction of hair growth over the body. These whorls need to be opposing so the hair can move in symmetrical streams over the body, meeting at lines or at tuft whorls where opposing symmetry is also achieved.

As in horses, dogs have places we always expect to find whorls, including the backs of elbows, on the chest, and under their bellies. Not finding a whorl in those locations or to find unmatched whorls are sure signs of issues.

Most commonly, whorls will be clockwise on the left side of a dog's body and counter-clockwise on the right. This can be affected by the length and thickness of the hair coat or by the animal's sex.

For example, female dogs tend to have counterclockwise whorls under their necks, just behind the jaws. Males are more likely to have clockwise whorls in the same area. One theory on the cause of this whorl pattern is that there are different hormone concentrations between male and female fetuses. Also, dogs with short-haired coats had significantly more whorls on each elbow.

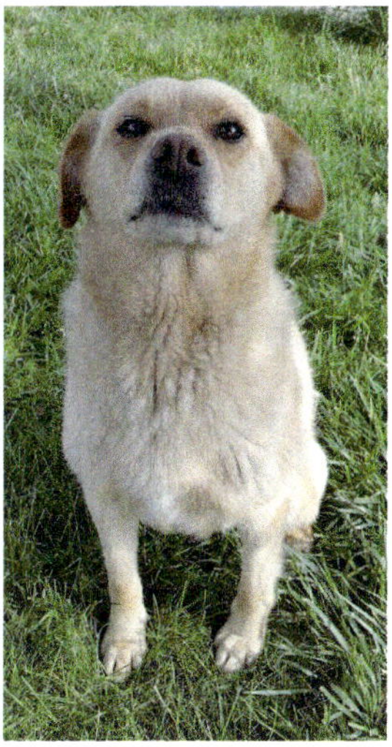

But what does that tell us about individual dogs?

There haven't been as many studies on dog whorls as there have been horse and cattle whorls, but there are a few.

Those studies have found correlation between a large number of counterclockwise whorls with high energy and excitable dogs. While reactivity in itself is not necessarily a problem, a higher state of reactivity or arousal can be a problem for some owners. Behavioral issues are the main reason listed when dogs are given up to shelters.

Chest whorl position seems to be a good indicator of temperament in dogs. Shelter dogs that were used in the studies had significantly more hair whorls on the chest than non-shelter dogs. Shelter dogs also tended to have chest whorls farther away from the 'thoracic inlet' (loosely speaking, the point of the chest) than non-shelter dogs.

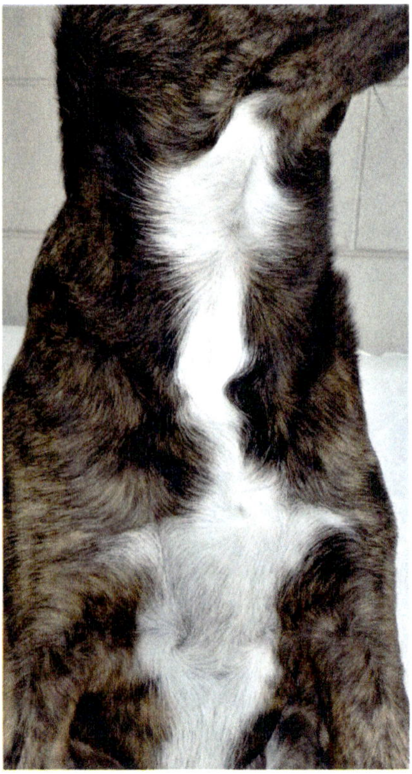

This dog has multiple chest whorls, with an extra one higher towards the neck in a counter-clockwise direction. She is not a shelter dog, but is described as crazy by her loving owner. She is sensitive and wary, with a tendency to bite first and ask questions later. Extremely attached to her owner, she is an all around good dog, just different.

One area where whorls and temperament have been studied is in the world of guide dogs.

Producing a guide dog is an expensive, time-consuming task. Especially when less than half of the dogs who enter guide dog programs complete them successfully, the others drop out because of health or behavioral issues. Finding a way to tell which dogs are a good fit before entering the program could save a lot of trouble for everyone involved.

It has been found that right-brain dogs, dogs who are reactive, fearful, easily distracted or excited, don't do as well in the training programs. One method of telling if a dog was dominant right or left-brain was to give them a food toy to interact with. Dogs who play with the toy using both paws or their left paw were less likely to complete training.

Dogs who tend to reach first with their right paw were found to be left-brain, curious, brave, and focused on the job at hand.

Another indicator of a dog who was left-brain and might successfully complete the program was the direction of the chest whorl.

Sixty-one percent of dogs with a counter-clockwise chest whorl were able to complete training.

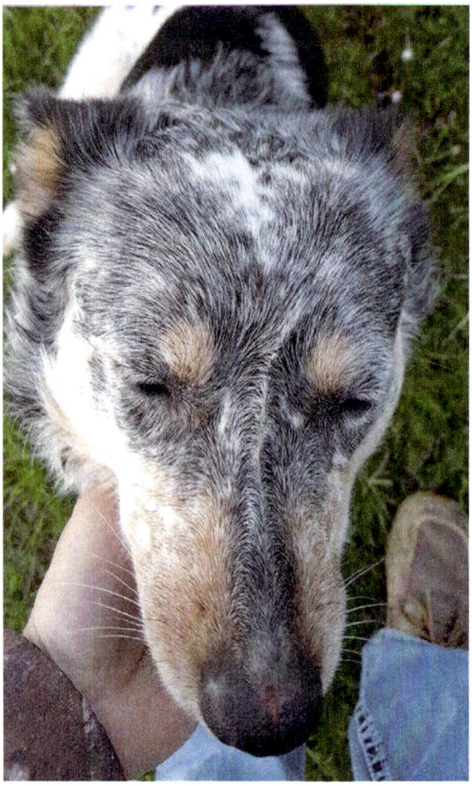

The meaning of this interesting whorl is unknown. She is a great dog, well-loved by her owners. She was hard to house train, is aggressive toward strangers, and timid around loud noises. How much of that is whorl related?

FLD Henry, who graduated the Future Leader Dog program, is working with a young Canadian man and currently accompanying him at grad school in Wales.

Areo, on the far left, was the only one of these three who made it in a career as a guide dog. FLD Shereman, in the center, was medically career changed at seven. Gus, on the far right, was career changed due to body sensitivities.

Having a way to tell which dogs are more likely to handle such a demanding, important job before investing so much time and money would be a great help.

It seems unlikely that a whorl could predict a medically caused career change, but body sensitivity is something that would go with a temperament type. If we could recognize the whorls and maybe even head types that go with a very sensitive temperament, a lot of stress could be avoided.

Whorls In People

Of course, people have whorls too. We usually notice them as that obnoxious spot where your hair refuses to lay flat.

There are many theories on the meanings behind whorls in people. Superstition has been passed down just like with horses. Like doubled whorled horses, there is one belief that a person with a double whorl will be quick-tempered and stubborn.

It is often said that the direction of whorls in people will show handedness. This is only loosely true. In many studies, it has been found that although the vast majority of right-handed people have clockwise whorls, half of all non right-handed people, left-handed and ambidextrous, have counter-clockwise whorls.

The genetics behind handedness are unknown. It can be difficult to know how many people are actually born right-handed. Many natural left-handed people have been taught to use their right hand because it is expected in schools or culture.

Up to one-half of children born to parents who are left-handed have been found to be right-handed. In identical twins the majority share handedness. There are less than a quarter of identical twins who are differently handed. Handedness is a complex trait influenced by the environment and genetics; a classic nature vs. nurture question as yet undecided by scientists.

Looking at whorls is fun, but they are not a concrete answer in this case. People are all unique, and it is difficult to find proof to backup beliefs and superstition relating to whorls.

It can be interesting to look at medically and scientifically proven cases where the hair on the outside of the body gives clues to medical conditions within. It helps build the case that whorls can be clues to temperament or muscle issues.

Spina Bifida Occulta is one such example. This is a condition where the spinal canal is open to varying degrees along the back, and a sac with part of the spinal cord will sometimes extend out through the skin. This exposes the spinal cord to injury and infection, and it can severely impact a person's mobility. This is one case where no one doubts the correlation between hair and the inner workings of the body.

Doctors are taught to look for a tuft of hair at the base of the spine to check for this developmental anomaly. Called a faun's tail, this patch of hair can be present from birth.

Interestingly along with a lack of folic acid during pregnancy, one of the possible causes of Spinal Bifida Occulta is the mother having a high fever during pregnancy. This is also common in foals born with a double forelock.

Prader-Willi Syndrome is a genetic cause of obesity in adults and failure to thrive in newborns. It is generally inherited from the father, who won't show symptoms. Children with Prader-Willi Syndrome will seldom cry, be generally sleepy, and have trouble eating.

Signs of Prader-Willi Syndrome include pale hair and skin, distinct facial features and pattern of hair whorls. These are all the same things we are looking at in horses to tell temperament and physical issues.

The whorl that accompanies Prader-Willi Syndrome is an upswept cowlick in the frontal hairline, above and between the eyes.

Whorl Examples

The best way to get a feel for reading whorls is by practicing, of course!

Here are a few examples to show how you need to look at the whole horse in order to get a clear picture.

Sometimes pictures can be easier than having the horse in front of you, as long as they are good clear pictures that show everything you need to see. With the horse there, you have other things to think about, like what the horse is doing, and what people with you are doing. There's always commotion and things going on near horses. It's a wonderful place to be, but not great for quiet contemplation.

A close-up picture of the head from the front and the sides are a good starting point. Pictures of whorls on the head and body should be close enough that you can see the whorls, and others far enough back that you can clearly see the position of the whorl. Conformation shots are also very helpful to see how whorls in areas like the base of the neck relate to the shape of the body.

Clear pictures from the front and side are important for getting a good idea of a horse's head shape and whorls.

When you have the proper pictures, find a quiet place, take a deep breath, and let the horse talk to you. What do you feel when you look at their head? Is there tension around the eyes or mouth that tells you he is nervous? How are his ears held? We aren't attempting to be psychic or do any mind-reading. We are simply getting a feel for the horse, taking in the emotions he is projecting. A horse's body language can tell us very clearly about them if we take the time to look.

We need to go slow and get a feel for the whorls and head shape. It seems simple and plain, but whorls can be deceptive, and head shapes sometimes seem to morph the longer we look at them.

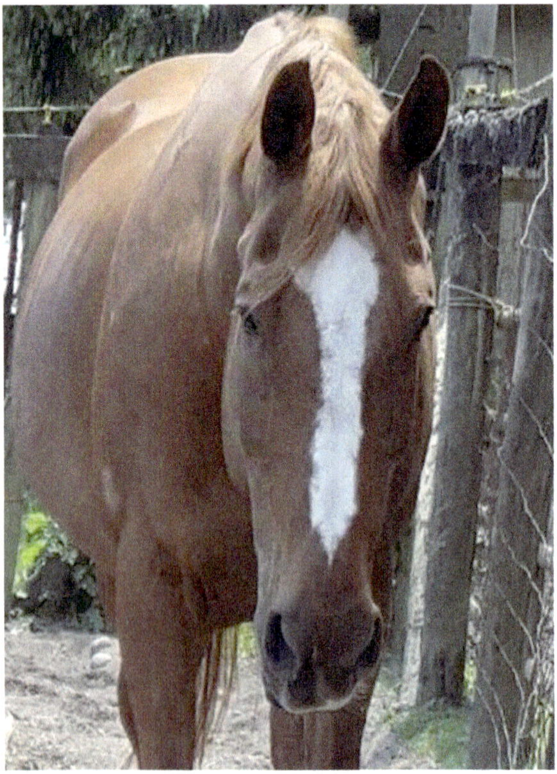

Copasetic

Jill, who rides Copasetic for ranch work, says that he was started by someone without much horse starting experience, and they did great together. That person didn't have any trouble riding him.

She got him and started using him for ranch work. After a light tuneup, he worked fine for her too. However he had a few issues, he'd run off occasionally and sometimes try to buck. He wasn't usually serious about the bucking, though, and always tried to get along.

Being a ranch horse, and not a personal horse, Jill wasn't able to keep him just for her and he was taken to be used for another rider. After that rider was unable to handle him Copasetic received some rough riding to 'fix' the bucking issues. That rider left him sore and bloodied, but not bucking.

Not at the moment, at least.

Back with Jill again, Copasetic got some time off to recover and a restart. After that experience, he wanted to buck anytime he was worked with and was very tight, unable to bend. He wanted to drop behind the bit and was constantly worried.

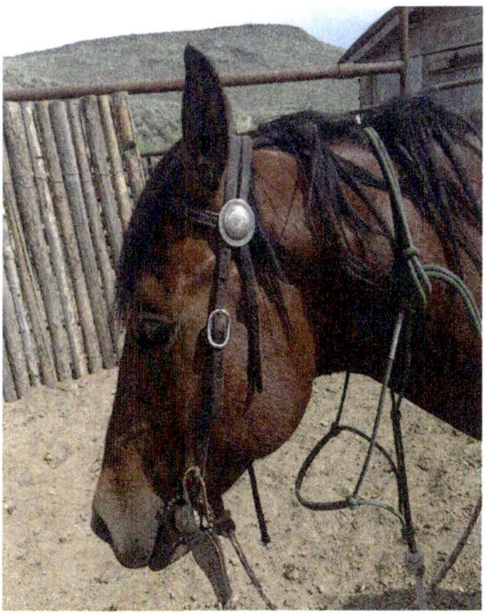

We can see Copacetic's willing head, straight square profile, and large jowl. If we only looked at this picture we would never guess the full story.

Built decidedly downhill, Copasetic comes to a V at the withers. This makes it difficult for him to use his body effectively. The underside of his neck is heavily muscled, while there is little muscling on the upper neck.
We would expect to see this body type in a horse with an open splaying whorl on the base of the neck.

An open splaying whorl like this draws a horse down onto the forehand. It usually accompanies low neck emergence from the shoulders.

The top of this whorl is off-center and to the right. It then connects with the left chest whorl at the base, which causes him to constantly pull to the left.
With the chest whorl and flank whorl combined, Copasetic is almost completely unable to bend to the right.

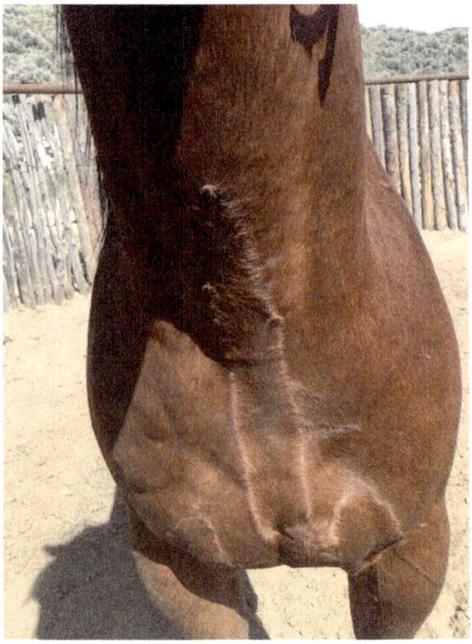

The whorl on the right side of his poll is set farther back than the one on his left, which would normally cause him to bend right. It is a small difference and not enough to counteract the rest of his body. His mane falls mostly to the left, and his left flank whorl breaks and restarts.
Both of these show a horse who will want to turn left.
His chest whorl pulls him to the left and onto the forehand, and the break in the flank whorl adds to it. All of this creates a body that is incapable of responding easily to the demands made of it.
A left-brain introvert will often buck when forced and uncomfortable.
Combining the body type and personality types, it isn't surprising that he bucked when forced to do work that he wasn't physically capable of.

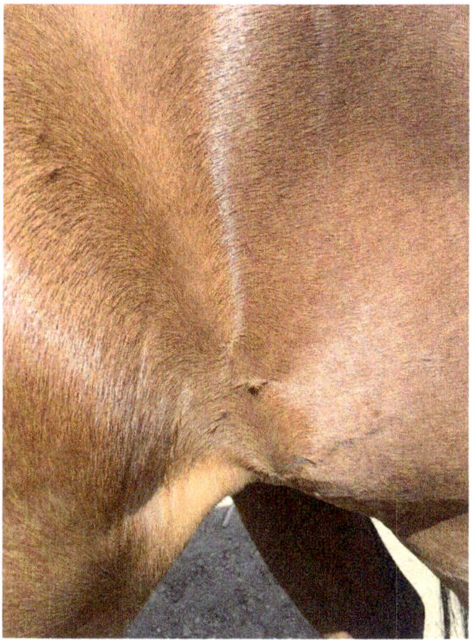

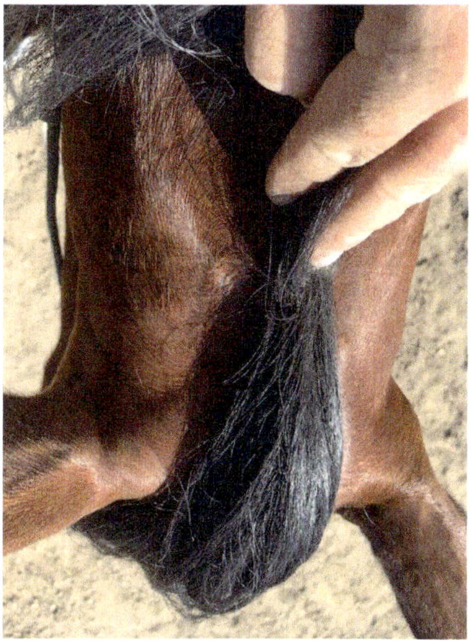

Dakota

When she first arrived at Lisa's stable, Dakota was charging and kicking at anyone who approached, and screaming constantly.

Lisa noticed her whorls and checked Linda Tellington-Jones' book on whorls. Working with her whorls and personality type, Lisa was able to recognize that Dakota was attacking out of pure terror. No one wanted to mess with this crazed horse, and she was left in her stall unattended. Dakota was a mess, and so was her stall.

Getting permission to work with her, Lisa managed to stay safe and help her to calm down. Lisa learned never to fight with Dakota and instead to stop and let her calm down when things became too much for Dakota to handle.

Lisa's training worked, and Dakota became safe enough for other people to handle and even to start riding. Dakota was sold and returned quickly, then sold again. This time she wasn't returned but sold to yet another home.

Once Lisa was in a position where she could buy a horse, she went looking for Dakota and was able to bring her home at last. For the most part Dakota was able to be handled safely by then, but was still scared and would attack when pushed too far.

Unfortunately, Dakota had to be put down due to injury, but got to spend the last of her time at peace in a home where she was loved.

Dakota is a perfect example of nature versus nurture.

She has a nearly perfectly straight profile that should indicate steady and calm.

She is a double whorl so she can be expected to be sensitive and a bit changeable when handled poorly. However, there are no reasons that can be seen in her profile or whorls to cause her to act the way she did.

Abuse can affect behavior strongly, and we need to be careful that we aren't blaming whorls for bad handling a horse has received in life.

Highland Mare

This young Highland mare has had a rough life. She went through five dealers before she reached thirteen months old, and she was skin and bone. Her face bears the scars of cigarette burns, and she had an understandable fear of people.

She is fat and happy now, in a wonderful loving home but still something is a bit off about her. Her owner swears she is not 'smart'.

She will pounce on and kill small animals that have the misfortune of being in her pasture. That is common enough, but this mare also eats them! The owner has seen it happen, and they have found animal bones in her poop.

Despite all of that, she is described as loyal.

More like a dog than a horse, she is very much a one person horse. Her owner says "Other people can handle her safely etc., but she'd rather it be me. I have spine issues, and I can sit on the floor resting against her legs, and she will stay there until I'm ready to get up and move." She is playful, affectionate, and friendly despite what she has suffered in life.

Her whorl is high, usually a sign of intelligence, a very active mind, and a quick learner.

Does that mean the whorls are wrong? Is she not smart, or does she show her intelligence unusually?

The effects of abuse and starvation on a horse's mind are incredible. We already know these things have terrible effects throughout life. She persevered and her natural intelligence is showing in unexpected ways, such as the eating of small things when she's bored.

That may not seem like an act of intelligence, but smart beings come up with something to keep them entertained when bored and alive when starving. Horses have no concept of cruelty, they only see the fun of the game.

It could be that she is just a unique and interesting individual. Smart in some ways, not so much in others. I think we all feel that way sometimes.

Looking at her pictures, we see that her eyes are set very high on her head. In some of the pictures it looks like she has a very short, broad head that doesn't taper much to the nose. There is a bit of a bulge below her eyes on her very broad, pronounced nose bone.

Those are all signs of a horse that might need a little extra time to figure things out.

She also has widely spaced ears that show her to be very steady. Her whorl is high, usually a sign of a very active mind.

Her whorl is to the left as we face her, making her a left brain horse; a fast learner, and playful.

She appears to be a very smart horse who was determined to stubbornly cling to life in the only way she knew how. Old habits can be hard to break, especially when those habits kept her alive.

Artie

Artie has some very unique whorls right on top of his head. Are they ear whorls or poll whorls? It can be so hard to classify these patterns sometimes

According to his trainer Artie "is VERY smart, too smart"!

Of course, we would expect that with his other whorls. He has a high double whorl, very smart, very focused. The whorls there are interesting too. They are longer and stretched, unlike a typical double whorl or a feathered whorl.

He also has a tendency to head shyness. From most people, I would put that down as poor handling. His person is an excellent trainer though, and would have long since dealt with the issues surrounding Artie's head shyness if they were simple.

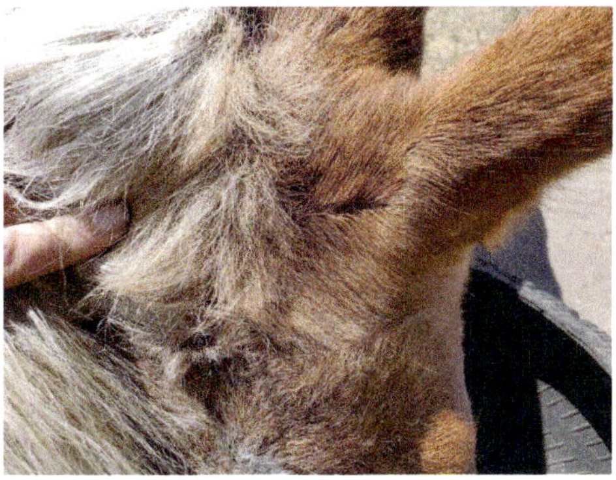

Whorls on the polls should show some sort of focus on the top of the head, such as head shyness. Extreme intelligence would be another trait poll whorls could be a sign of.

His trainer also says, "He has a strong personality and definitely has two 'sides'. He is a saint with his kid and people he likes/that he meshes well with. He is stubborn, willful and challenging for the vet and people he doesn't like or mesh well with. He's incredibly smart and inquisitive. When he came here, he was quite shut down and a 'hop to it horse,' so he seemed a bit flighty and reactive. With the use of positive reinforcement in his training, he's settled to being quiet but highly responsive."

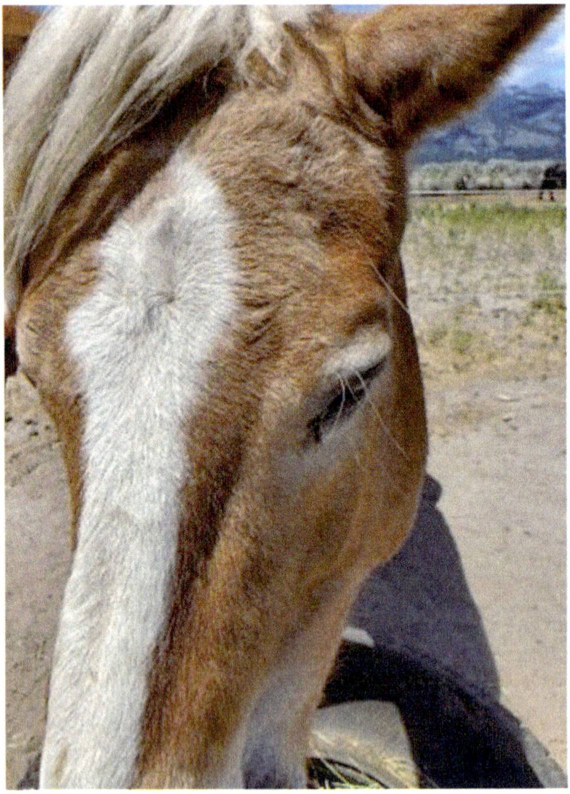

Artie's forehead whorls are not feathered, instead, they have a big loose whorl that shows a lack of focus.

His high double whorl shows his intelligent, job focused, and brave personality this is only slightly dulled by his general lack of focus.

The whorl on Artie's neck is not open and splaying. Instead, it is ridge shaped. The hair comes together and overlaps rather than pulling away from each other, a zipper whorl. Artie is built uphill, and although he is upright at the base of the neck, he tends to arch over his whorl.

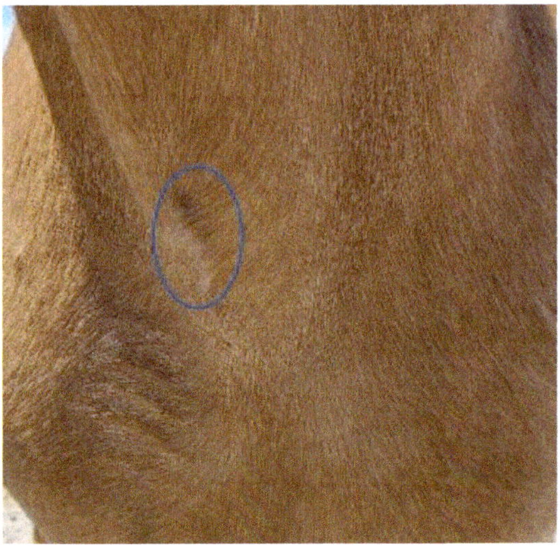

Artie has a single whorl on his right jaw. Jaw whorls show a horse who is a thinker, who can think up all sorts of trouble with their very active minds. They are curious and clever, very friendly and can be pushy.

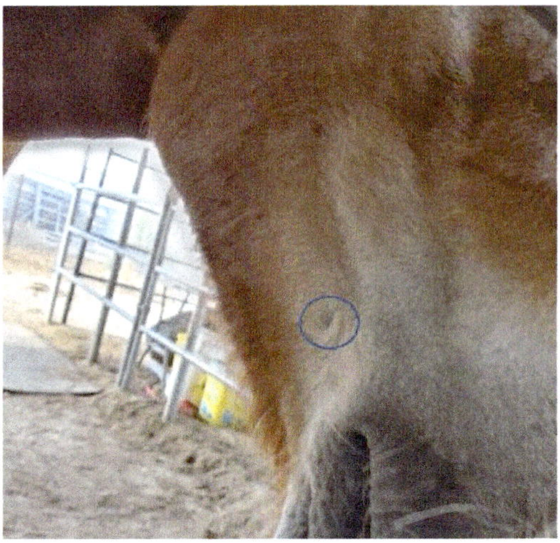

Sorrel Mare

This mare has diagonal double whorls, which are sometimes referred to as the dreaded Z pattern. In the tradition of the Z pattern, she has been rejected by dozens of trainers. The last one said she was psycho. She nearly killed her owner.

Is this proof that horses with the Z pattern are dangerous? Quite the opposite in fact. After being sent to a lady who trains in a kinder, more understanding style, she has turned around and become a sweet loving horse. The new trainer gave this mare a chance to have more choice and control in her training and that made all the difference.

Everyone loves to work with her. She learns quickly and easily, and is eager to train. This is a case of a horse being misunderstood and her pleas for help ignored.

A right-brained introvert, she appears to be quiet and not worried by the things going on around her or being done to her. Her calming signals are subtle and easy to miss when we don't pay attention.

Her ears are long and narrow, showing some tendency to be unpredictable. They are set wide apart though countering the unpredictability with steady willingness.

After she has given many warning signs and been ignored, she lashes out in self-defense, and we perceive it as something out of the blue. She holds her feelings inside so much that she will bring herself to colic before she finally can't handle it anymore and explodes. This isn't a horse who is unpredictable and dangerous, this is a horse who needs to be listened to and have her voice heard. When people are willing to do so, she is safe, willing, and happy.

The new trainer took a lot of time and taught her to escalate her reactions more slowly. This was achieved by being ultra-sensitive to her slightest uncertainty and reinforcing her for using quieter and more subtle forms of calming signals. Then, anything that was worrying the mare was removed. This trainer built up communication so the mare could tell people when she was worried instead of exploding.

This photo shows her large eyes set far apart on a broad forehead marked by pronounced brain muscle. Everything about her head screams intelligence and sensitivity. Her nostrils are large and open with the tips pulled back, showing a horse who is alert and often disturbed by the actions of people around her. Some might say they are wrinkled in disgust.

Lusitano Mare

This mare tends to intimidate people who have to work with her. She scares farriers and body workers with her desire to be in charge and her taste for drama. Her owner has become accustomed to braiding a rearing horse.

Despite her reputation as a handful, she is solid as a rock and quite happy to be ridden once she is out where the action is. There was no trouble at all starting her under saddle, perhaps because she always wants to be the center of attention, her owner muses.

Ridiculously smart, she can open gates, line up rocks along the top of a fence, and climb inside water troughs. A favorite pastime in the pasture is to buck next to an apple tree so that the top of her butt hits a big branch and apples come raining down on her head.

A high center whorl with feathering, combined with her convex nose, shows a left-brained horse. She is very smart, which is emphasized again by the width between her eyes and her refined muzzle. Left-brained horses like to think of ways to amuse themselves. They see no reason not to demand whatever they want and can be pushy about getting their way.

Whorls in the girth area were once thought to be a sign of good luck, according to superstition. Now we only see them as another reason to be polite when tightening the girth.

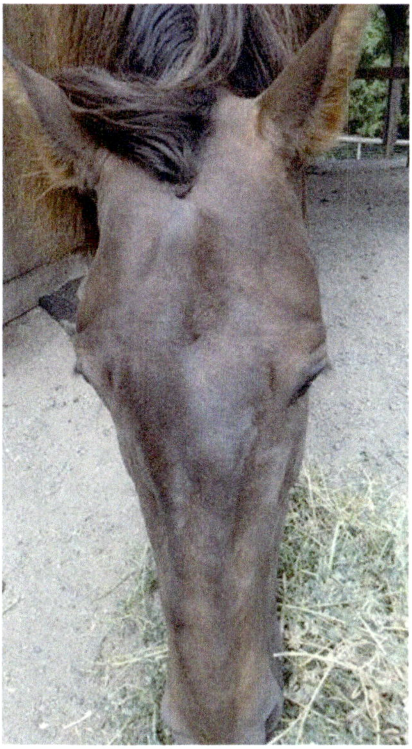

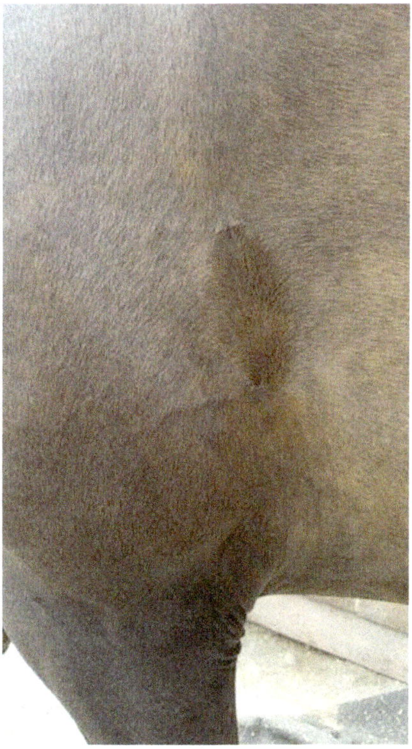

Kayden

When Tannesha first went to look at Kayden, he ran away with her and nearly threw her over a hundred-foot drop into a ravine. She bought him anyway. After they had time to settle in together, Kayden became a trustworthy mount, beloved by children and adults alike.

Kayden also turned out to be a hermaphrodite. He possess both male and female genitalia. They decided to refer to him as 'he' because he seemed happier to answer to that than to 'she'.

Kayden also has an enlarged heart.

Is there any way we could tell Kaydens unique traits from his whorls?

A high single whorl, placed slightly to the right as we face him, marks him as a right-brained extrovert. Combined with a very straight profile and square muzzle, he will be both alert and emotional, yet calm and trustworthy.

Kayden does have some unique whorls that could give us hints as to his inner workings. It would take several more horses with whorls and characteristics like Kayden's to make comparisons and find similarities before we could settle on any theories. Still, it is interesting to observe what whorls he displays and wonder about their meanings.

On his chest, Kayden has several small whorls. Are these related to the heart problems?

Above his flank, Kayden has an extra whorl. Could this be related to his extra sexual organs?

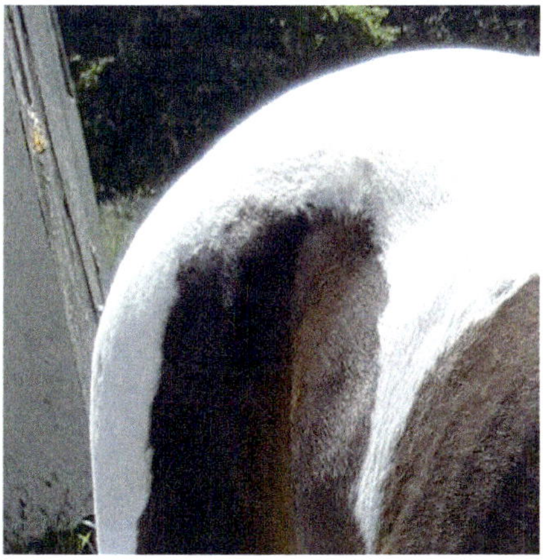

Eugene

Eugene is a Thoroughbred Connemara cross. His owner got him after taking an Andalusian to fourth level in dressage, and she was hoping to bring him along in the same manner.

He likes to travel with his back hollow and head high, on constant alert. His owner has become frustrated trying to get him to go round as he instead wants to pop his head and neck up and fall over the right shoulder while traveling in both directions. Long and low is the best he has to offer. He tends to explode, especially when tracking left. With a tendency to over bend to the right, he will bend left with some difficulty. It is a sign of her skill that he is as well-muscled as he is.

After looking for eyesight issues with his right eye due to his cranial asymmetry, his owner finally concluded that the problem was simply that he was physically unable to do the work asked of him so she took a closer look at his whorls.

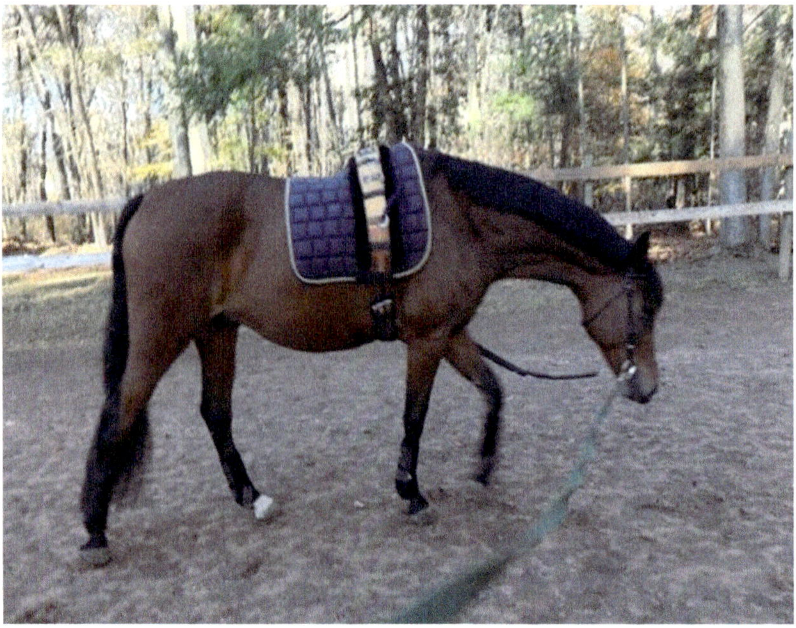

Eugene should be a left-brained extrovert with his high left whorl. What could cause him to be explosive instead of brave and confident?

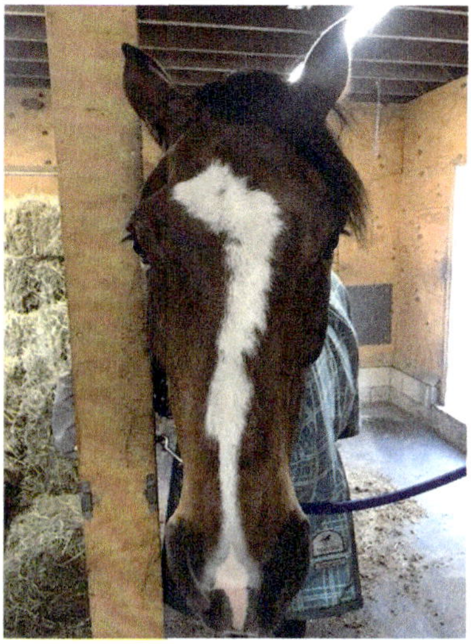

If we look at the entire head, his zygomatic arch on the right side is dropped and back, his right ear is dropped, his atlas is tipped right, and his whole head is shifted down on the right side.

His neck has a single whorl on the right combined with an open splaying whorl on the bottom left. These whorls combined, would cause an extreme right curve and throw him off balance.

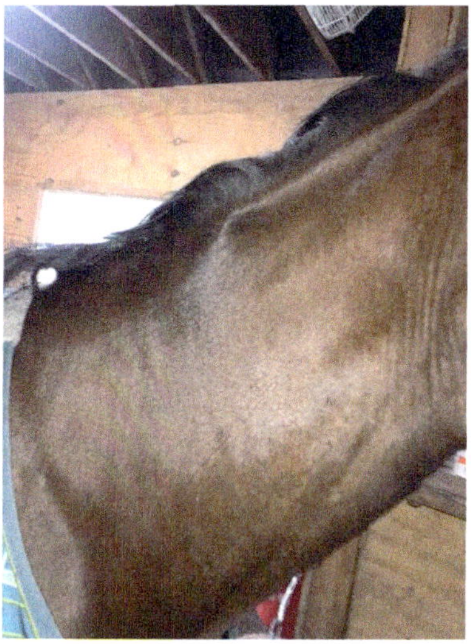

When combined with the lack of symmetry in his head, we get a horse who is trying his best to do as asked but is betrayed by a body that won't cooperate.

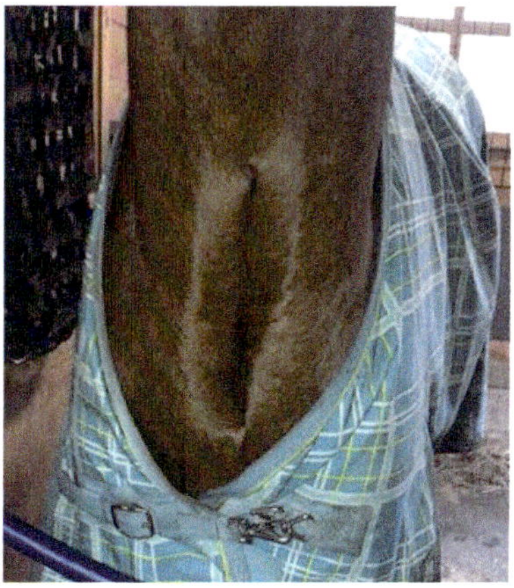

Charlie

Charlie is a great example of the power nurture has over nature.

He was bought off a meat truck at fifteen months old, along with thirteen other colts, one of them was only three months old. The lady who bought them turned them out to pasture where they lived mostly wild until Charlie was three.

Mitch brought the freshly gelded Charlie home, where he had to learn to interact with humans and adult horses, unlike the young herd he grew up in. The transition was difficult for him. He showed a strong tendency to rear, paw, and spook.

Mitch began to suspect that some of his difficulty and behavioral issues were from eye issues and had him checked. The vet confirmed he had a cataract over the lens of his left eye and that he was probably born that way due to lack of nutrition.

During a recent massage, the massage therapist discovered a build-up of muscle by his left shoulder. The massage therapist said she suspected it was from carrying his head turned to the left to allow him to see with his good eye.

Despite his bad start, Charlie is now a very sweet and loving pony. Although spooky, he is curious, and after a spook, he will face the object and then go and check it out. With continued training he is learning to learn and loves to work with Mitch.

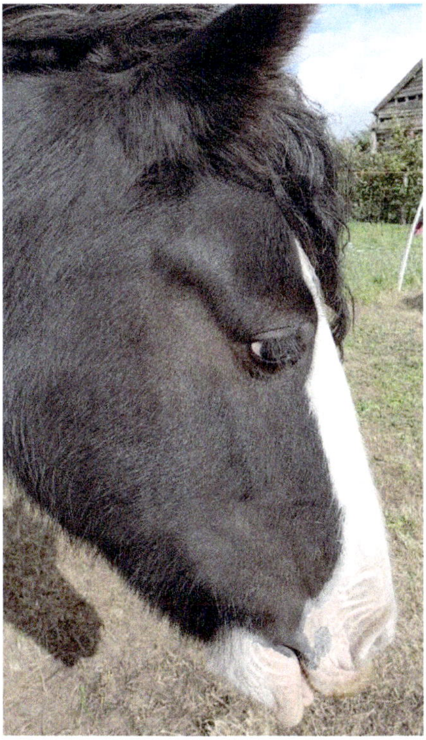

Looking at Charlie's head from the side, we see a mostly straight profile showing a hint of a convex curve. He should be steady, tough, and left-brained. His chin is soft and uncomplicated. That dip between his nostrils above his upper lip means he should be very smart.

From the front, we can see a basic single center whorl beneath all that hair. A center whorl doesn't show us a whole lot; it means he pulls from the four quarters of his brain with no extremes in any direction.

We need to look at the rest of the head for clues to his temperament. His eyes are fairly far apart but not noticeably wide. His ears are shapely and fairly far apart.

And of course, we can't overlook that mustache!

All of that points to a calm, easy-going horse.

By all apparent signs, he should be a quiet, easy-going fellow, and he tries so hard to be.

Between a rough, wild start to life and partial sight in his right eye, he has a tendency to be spooky and high-strung at times.

That doesn't mean his whorls and head shape lie. It only means that everything has an influence on how horses turn out in life. He is still a great well-loved horse, who is smart and willing. He happily tries his best at everything that is asked of him.

Ghost

Ghost was an orphaned calf raised on a bottle. Retained as a heifer and all-around pet, Ghost loves learning tricks and will hopefully become a riding cow.

She is an enthusiastic learner, smart, and quick to pick up new lessons. Full of energy, Ghost is not quiet and by no means a dead head. That doesn't mean that she is spooky, just exuberant.

She doesn't fight in the chute and moves easily with the rest of the herd. In this case, it is hard to tell how much is nature and how much is nurture. After very recently giving birth, Ghost is proving to be a wonderful mother.

At first glance, it would appear that Ghost has a simple single whorl placed nicely between the eyes. On closer inspection though she has two more at the corner of each eye.
In a horse, three whorls would mean quiet, the born broke type, but quirky.

She also has a whorl at each temple. In a horse, this would show a very quick learner who figures problems out quickly and a thinker who creates their own games.

So far, this does seem to apply to her.

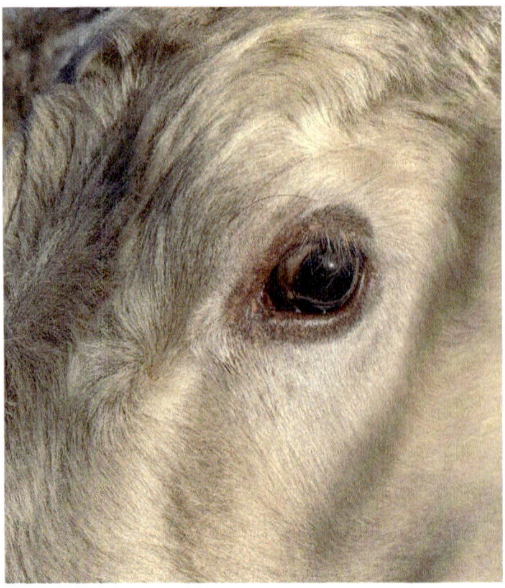

Harvey

Harvey found himself in a kill pen about to ship. He had been used up and dumped. Scarred from pin firing, his legs were not entirely sound. That combined with being in abject terror and trembling in fear when people got near, he had no hope of finding a home.

Saved by a rescue almost on accident, Harvey had his road shoes pulled and got to spend a year on pasture being a horse. He still didn't want to be caught or to have anything to do with humans.

Once in a home where he was regularly worked with, Harvey began to see humans as friends instead of something to be feared. Now he wants to be a puppy dog and cuddle on your lap. He is still very emotional, but begging to be loved instead of cowering in fear.

Because he is being worked in a way that allows him to have a say and builds his confidence instead of punishing his fear, Harvey loves his training. He comes running in from pasture instead of being hard to catch. He will still spook, but comes running back immediately after recovering from his start.

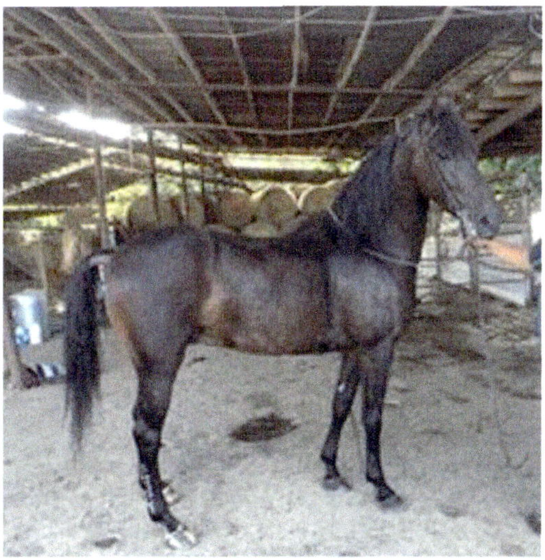

Harvey in the sale barn, reacting to the overwhelming stimuli in the way any right-brained extrovert would, with fear and flight.

From the side, we can see a mostly straight profile. Harvey has a long head that narrows considerably to the muzzle. That will make him sensitive and a quick learner.

His jowl isn't huge; it is about medium sized, average. It shows an average learning ability. His chin is soft and round, he wants to get along and is very willing.

Harvey has very hard nervous eyes. They show how worried he is about life.

From the front, we see a head that is long from ears to nose, and he isn't broad between the eyes. Again, he wants to get along and to be friends. He needs clear instruction, though, or he will be overwhelmed and get extremely nervous.

His whorl is high and slightly to our right, showing a right-brained extrovert. Harvey is emotional and reactive. Combined with the rest of his head, we get a horse who needs a lot of love and reassurance. If forced or handled roughly, he will be overcome by nerves and be a spooky, reactive horse. With patience and understanding, he is a horse who tries his heart out and is desperate to please.

The head isn't the whole story, though.

As we look at the rest of Harvey's body, we see large open splaying chest whorls. The one on his left is slightly larger than his right. Harvey likes to paw as a nervous tick. He also uses his front legs the way a dog does. He will reach for things with them and use them almost like a tool. He has very high front leg action too.

His mane changes sides a few inches behind his ears, in the exact spot that his swan neck overarches. The swan neck leads to a hollow back even with his nose tucked.

That hollow back is also long and weakly coupled. All of this combines with terrible hind leg conformation that leaves him off balance and insecure in his movement. Is it a case of the bad conformation leading to insecurity and nervousness? Or are they two separate causes of nervousness but unrelated but working together?

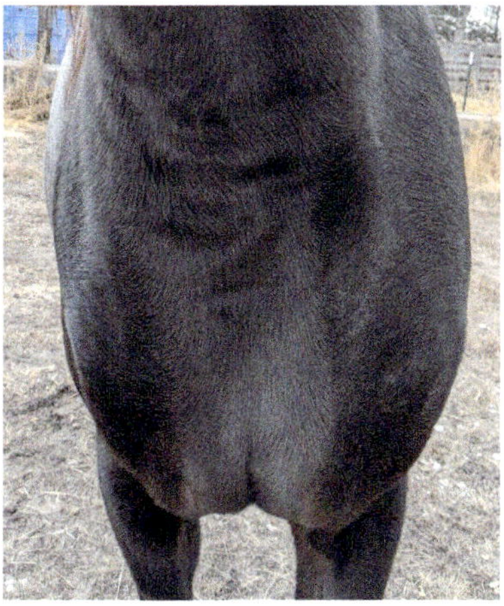

The Wee One or Wee Poquita

She has always been one for a title.

Her owner started The Wee One when she was a two year old. She was always super sensitive and reactive to the point that Jill strongly disliked her and turned her down when Wee Poquita was offered as a thank you for training.

After some thought, Jill changed her mind and accepted The Wee One as a gift.

She still wasn't fond of this big yellow horse, and they fought constantly. For two years, The Wee One went everywhere at a jig. Oversensitive and spastic, The Wee One was very dramatic and easily upset. To the extent of randomly flipping over on top of Jill once as they were standing still one day. She had Jill at her wit's end.

Until Jill changed jobs and began working with a very skilled horseman. He complimented The Wee One as she and Jill danced and fought their way home.

That really struck home with Jill and she started looking for what he saw in this horse. Instead of fighting, Jill left The Wee One alone and let her figure out her job.

And she did!

While she is still a very quirky horse, The Wee One learned her job as a ranch horse so well that all Jill has to do is "stay aboard, open gates, and catch the critter with my rope and she'd do the work." She describes The Wee One as a high-powered animal that is extremely forward. Big motored, sensitive, and dramatic when corrected.

The Wee One has a broad forehead that is wide between the eyes and narrows considerably down to a very refined sensitive muzzle. Her eyes are large and clearly visible from the front.

The ears are almost straight up and curvy. All signs of intelligence, sensitivity, and lots of go!

Her nostrils are large with clear definition around them, showing that she is very alert and reactive.

Her upper lip is well defined and curious; she'll want to explore her world and check things out with her mouth.

The whorls get even more interesting, though. She has a single-centered whorl which is basic and normal for horses. But if we look high to our right, there is a second whorl, an outlier. She is centered by the first whorl but will show occasional extremes of far right-brained extrovert behavior, very smart, very reactive, very emotional.

Coyote

Hauled to an auction as a two-year-old, Coyote was an extremely ugly young Morgan when he was purchased by a very bad man. Luckily for him, someone saw the purchase and was horrified at the thought of this ugly baby going to that home. She offered the man more than he had paid, and the ugly duckling went home with Tammie. He was still with her and well-loved many years later when news came of the very bad man's arrest for a yard full of horses starved to death.

An accident-prone youngster, Coyote grew up to be an incredibly intelligent and opinionated horse. Willing to tolerate inexperienced riders on his back, he would pack them about carefully. When he didn't approve of what they did, he would make his disapproval very clear. Once, when he felt his cinch was tightened too much, too quickly, he threw himself to the ground in protest.

When bored he would spook at shadows, but he feared nothing when there was work to be done. Well-loved his entire life, Coyote was appreciated for his complex, difficult, and completely trustworthy character.

With an experienced rider, he was a handful and a delight to ride. He had ideas on how things should be done and, if left to do it himself, was quite capable alone. As a cow horse, he could work cattle all day with the reins left loose on his neck. Coyote always carried tension, displayed by his braced neck and tight mouth.

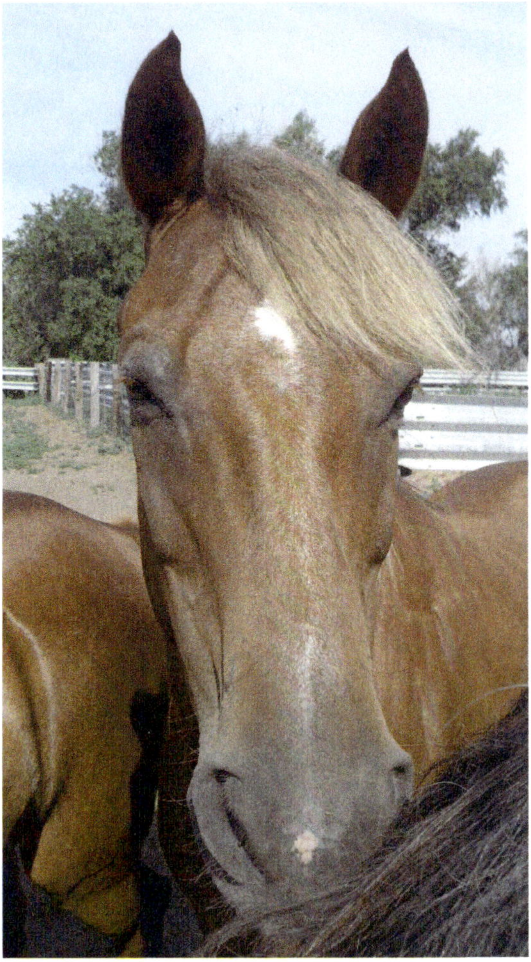

From the front, we can see wide-set ears that are very curvy and upright, smart and steady but energetic. Well defined brain muscle and stacked double whorls, changeable and sensitive. Coyotes nose bone is very well defined, he will have strong opinions.

His eyes are almond shaped, he isn't one to make friends easily, a bit standoffish. His nostrils are large and open. He is alert and aware of everything around him. His muzzle is rounded, he will only take orders if he feels they are worth following.

From the side, we can see his extremely tight complex chin. He carries lots of tension around his mouth and will be a very complex character, not an easy horse but a good one.

Former Bucking Horse

We don't know anything about this horse except that he didn't make it as a bucking horse and is being restarted in hopes of making a riding horse. So instead of telling his story, we will go straight to letting him tell us a story.

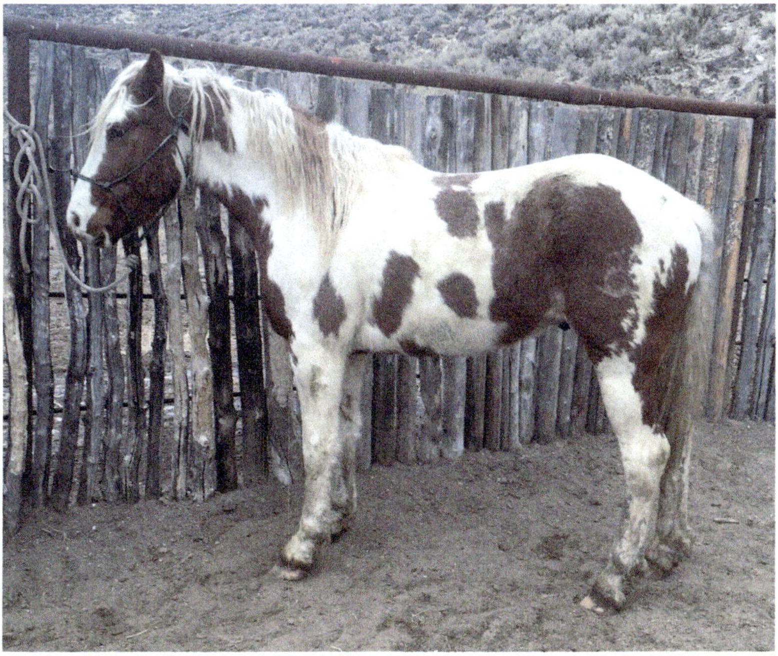

We can see the big thick legs typical of the draft crosses that are so popular as bucking horses. They have the powerful build capable of shaking any rider loose. But will he have the desire? Or will he be able to transition to riding instead?

He looks hopeful from the front. His ears are set wide at the base and even wider at the tips. They aren't overly curvaceous, he should be fairly steady, easy going, and willing.

His eyes aren't set very wide apart, suggesting that he may take longer to learn a lesson. That also means he won't be learning the wrong lessons all the time or thinking up new games on his own.

His whorl is high and slightly to our right. He is an extrovert and possibly a bit of a right brain extrovert. His eyes look slightly wary; he can be nervous and worry about things.

From the side, we can see a mostly straight profile. There may be a hint of a dish and a hint of a moose nose, showing he will be sensitive and bold. We already knew sensitive from his whorl and eyes. Hopefully the bold parts of his personality will stand out.

His chin is soft and kind. His mouth is very short. Bits may be uncomfortable and lessons may take awhile to learn. The head is thick, combined with being narrow in front, meaning, once again, he may take time to learn new things.

The tightly tufted neck whorl is where he will be upright through the neck then arch over the whorl. That part is good. We can see in the picture from the side that he has beautifully developed neck muscles. He looks good, until we get to the base of his neck where the whorl drifts off to the left of his chest.

The biggest problem with this horse is his chest. The chest whorls are terribly uneven, with a small tight whorl above the larger chest whorl on his right. His left whorl is small and tilts to the side away from center.

Everything else about this horse was looking promising. These whorls will make this horse travel terribly uneven. He will likely have trouble picking up anything other than his right lead. Discomfort in the body could also lead to behavioral issues.

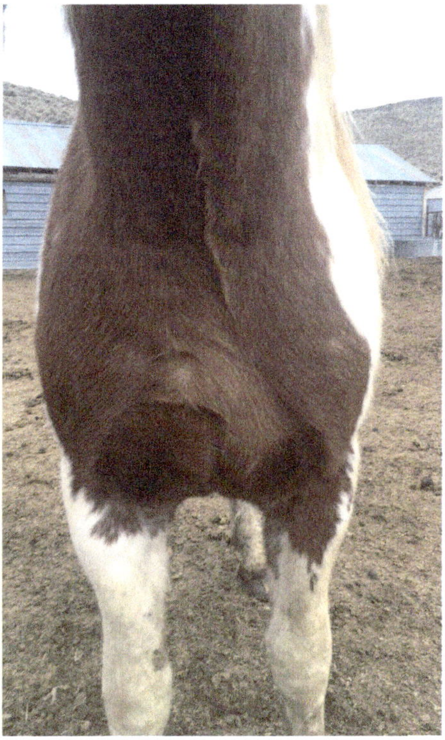

Mick

A nineteen-year-old warmblood, Mick has been plagued with health and behavioral problems most of his life. Sold by his breeder as a six year old, he went through eight homes in five years before landing with Maggie at eleven. He was lucky to find someone who was willing to search for solutions to his problems instead of passing him along again, and he is still with her.

When he first came into Maggie's life, he would put his head down and charge through anything in front of him. He dealt with difficulties in life by running. His vet thought he did it for the endorphin rush. He would blow out his stifle every time he was turned out, from racing so hard around the field. He also had a strangely tilted sternum, to add to his other health issues.

Part of his problem with running off was due to being so heavy on the forehand that he was unable to stop. Maggie recognized this and switched to only walking then found a trainer who specialized in rehabilitation of chronic lameness through re-coordination of the spine.

Mick rearing in protest to hand walking while being treated for encysted parasites and tapeworm.

A year into this walking work, his stifles were healed. Unfortunately, when trotting was re-introduced, Mick began leaping randomly into the air. After this bizarre behavior continued for some time, they tried treating for encysted parasites and tapeworm. He had them, bad.

It took over a year for Mick to recover from that. During that time, his shoes were removed, and Maggie began learning how awful his feet truly were. He is now barefoot and is trimmed carefully by Maggie, who learned how to trim to his very specific needs. As a result, he is doing better than ever, despite Navicular and ringbone issues.

All horses react differently to pain. Mick's response to the pain in his hooves and gut was extreme and violent. When he is perfectly comfortable, in his body and his training, he turns into a very quiet horse with more "whoa" than "go". He can be trusted to carry inexperienced riders for short periods and will be an ideal riding horse until he decides he is done. Then he is off and there is no stopping him. He is quite curious his first time to a new location. Maggie can take him on a trail ride bareback. Then he will outright refuse to leave again, trying to buck, rear, and bolt the whole time.

Mick working beautifully when everything is just right.

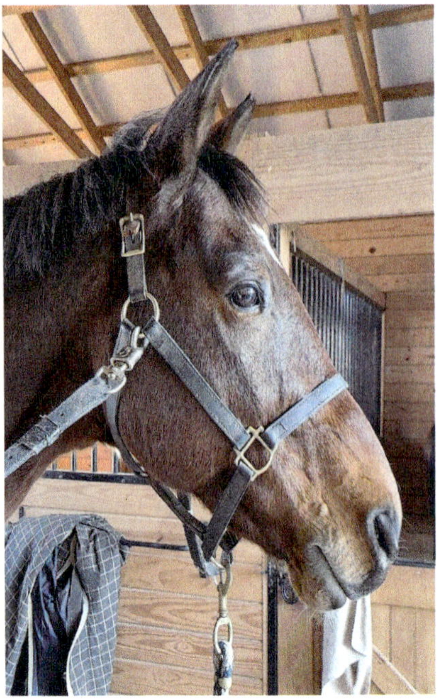

From the side, we see a straight profile, meaning steady. It ends with a rounded muzzle though, he is going to have his own ideas in life and may not learn new things easily or quickly.

His eyes are tight and round, no soft, kind eyes here. He will probably carry tension and anxiety.

His chin is soft and simple, he should be easy going.

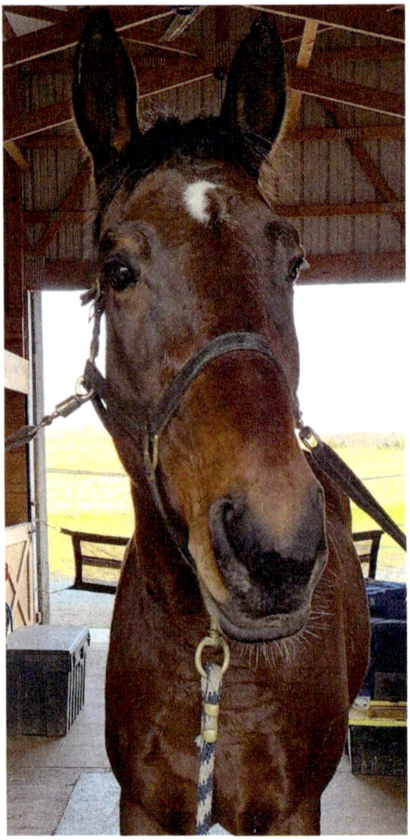

From the front, we see ears that are broad without much definition. Slightly wider at the top, they should show a horse who is willing and fairly steady.

His eyes are an average distance apart.

His upper lip is curious and interested, he will want to explore his world with it.

Mick's chest whorls are even and in the normal places.

He isn't looking overly complicated yet.

From up close, though, we can see the worry lines and wrinkles above his eyes showing stress, pain, or concern.

We can also see his whorl. It is surrounded by scratches and scuffs where the hairs have been scraped off.

He has a very clear single whorl positioned slightly to our right. From the whorl a line of feathering comes up and curves in an S-shape until it comes back to a ghost whorl to our left of his star.

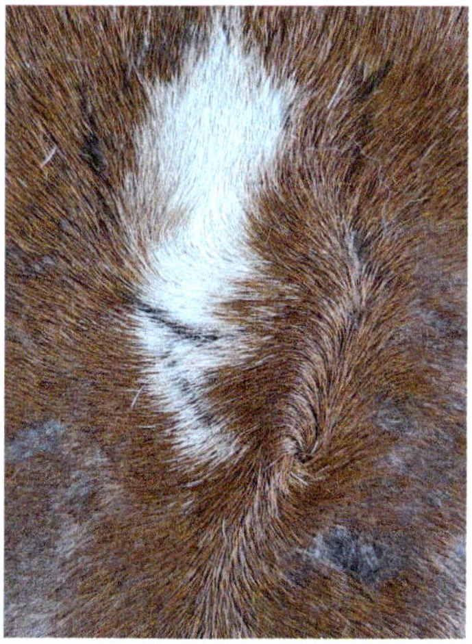

He is a diagonal double whorl.

S-shaped feathering often shows a horse who tends to get hurt regularly. Mick tends to run through things and get these little scrapes and scratches regularly.

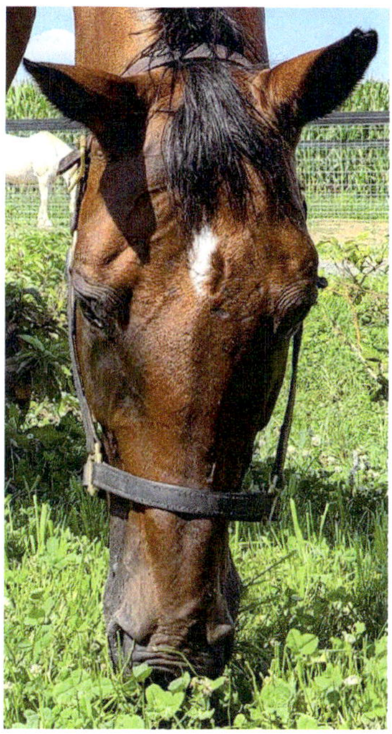

A diagonal double whorl tends to show an introverted horse, one who won't show fear or pain until they explode with it, seemingly out of the blue. Maggie says she would describe him as a right-brained extrovert at his worst and a left-brained introvert at his best.

He also has an unusual ridge of bone running up the center of his forehead. Any meaning to that ridge is unknown.

To top off Mick's diagonal double whorls, he has a large number of whorls under his neck. Most of them are set to his right. These small tight whorls will pull him to the right and make bending to the left difficult for him.

He has hi/lo syndrome in the front feet, with the left fore being very low while the right hoof is much higher. His sternum tilts down to the left as well. With the whorls creating tightness in his right side, we can picture how the pulling could produce such imbalance.

To make it even worse, he doesn't have a belly whorl on his left side.

The lack of a whorl on his belly combined with being pulled so hard to the right caused him to overcompensate by overextending the left hind leg clear under himself. Careful training has helped him correct the issue with his movement by evening out muscles, not reaching as far under with the left leg, and carrying himself better.

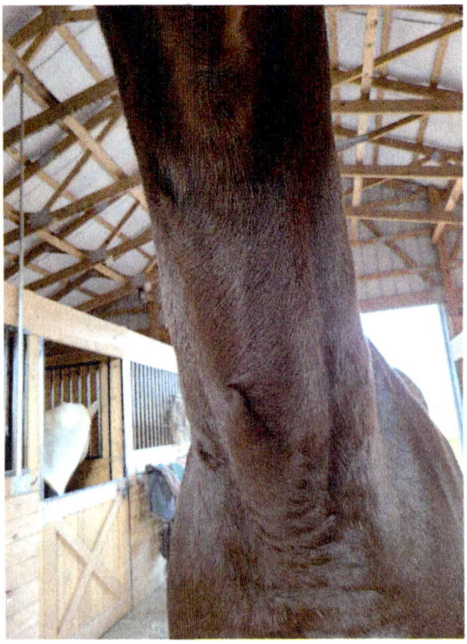

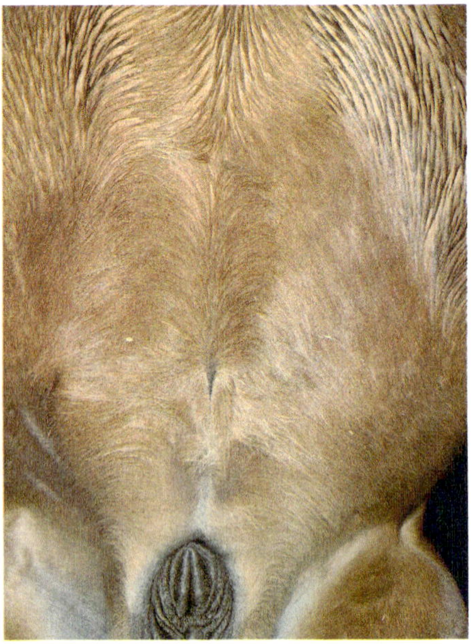

Comanche

Paula knew she wanted to keep Comanche when he was only a day old. His mom, Cheyenne, is one of her favorite cows because of her beautiful coloring and her personality. She had a reputation as being sassy when she was a calf. Paula likes cows with a little bit of attitude.

Comanche also had pretty coloring like Cheyenne. The pattern is called roan in cattle, just like it is in horses.

He has always been a big guy. He was born big and thick. Those big guys really do tend to be pretty easygoing. She says he's pretty chill and not much scares him. Although he's a very calm steer, he does have a "wild side" like his mom.

This past spring while she waited on the pasture to grow, Paula grazed her steers in the yard in the evenings. A few times, Comanche took off when he saw her walking up with the halter to put them back in for the night. The other steers didn't even try to avoid being caught.

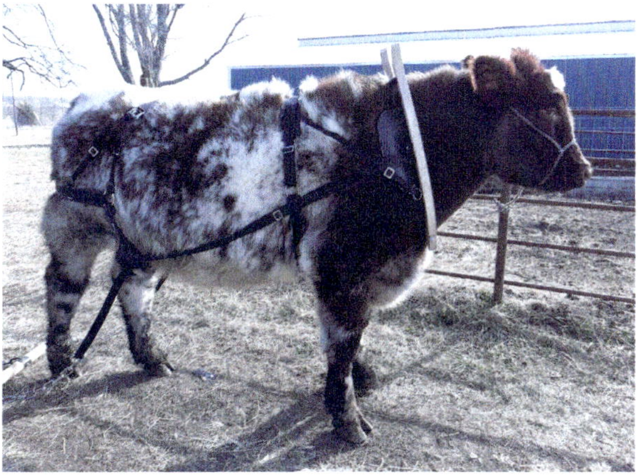

Comanche is in training to be a riding steer, to drive, and to pull like an ox. He is enthusiastic and willing in his training.

We can see that Comanche has had a docile dairy-type head from the time he was born. The main features don't change with age.

The same is true with his perfectly centered whorl.

He was a big calf and has matured into a big steer. Animals with bigger bone have been shown to have quieter more docile temperaments than animals with finer bone.

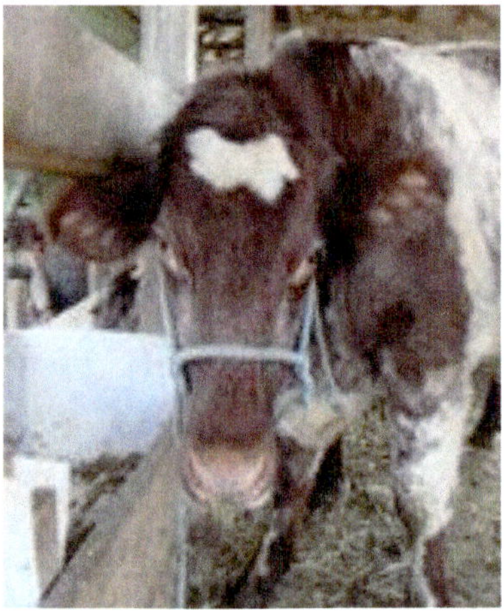

We would have no reason to expect anything less of him than to make a great working animal.

Steers will never stop growing, and Comanche is going to get huge!

Mongrel

Mongrel ran wild with a group of feral horses on the plains of Wyoming until he was full grown. First haltered in a chute, he bit and struck at the people attempting to work with him. Not wanting to mess with him, the first people passed him on to a lady who was willing to spend the time to overcome his extreme defensiveness.

For the first month, she would go into the pen with him and sit while they stared at each other for hours on end. Neither moving, just watching. Eventually, he overcame his fear of her, and they learned to work together.

Mongrel has never offered to buck. He is the most consistent horse she has ever ridden, always giving the exact same ride and response. That also means that he will stay scared of something if it bothers him, every single time.

He has a strong sense of self-preservation and will make sure that he and his rider are safe. Always willing, he wants to be brave, but needs support from his rider to maintain his bravery. He does his best to do anything asked of him.

Mongrel's one fear is people. He will do anything for his one trusted rider but is scared to even walk through groups of people. No one else is able to ride him.

Mongrel is a big boy. It's easy to see his mixed heritage of draft horses, mustangs, Thoroughbreds, and Morgans, combined with whatever else was turned out or escaped from neighboring ranches.

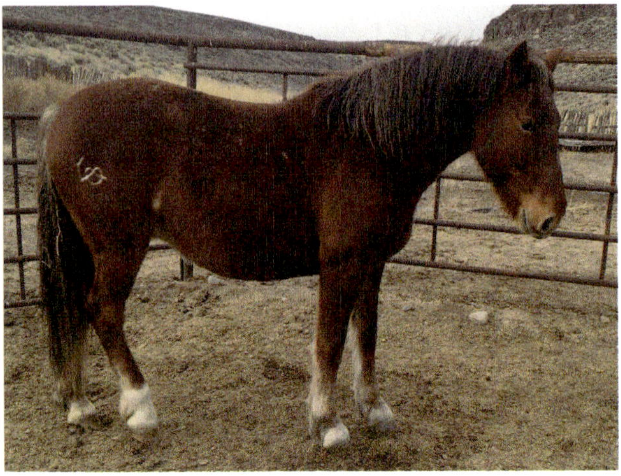

From the side, we can see Mongrel's strongly convex profile. Tough and determined, he will have his own ideas about life and how things should be done. He will also be able to power through any job and get done what needs done.

With his large jowl he won't run out of air. His chin is soft, showing a kind and willing horse.

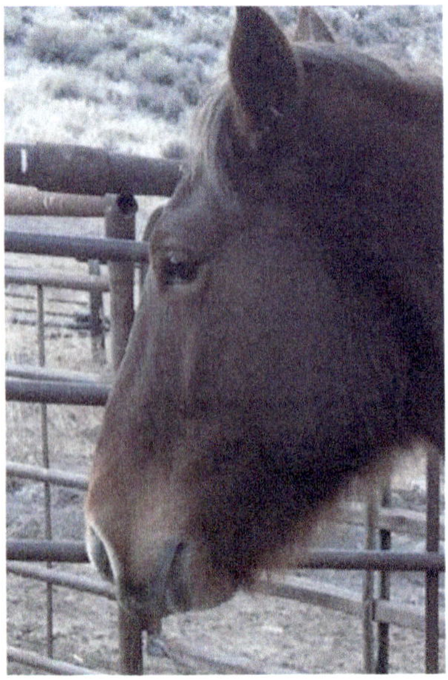

His mouth is short possibly making it difficult for him to carry a bit comfortably. In fact, he was not happy in a snaffle. Trained in bridle horse tradition, he carried his spade bit for a year without it being touched. This allowed him to become comfortable in it before it was used to signal. Now he works nicely in a bit.

From the front, we see a perfectly centered single whorl. That only tells us that we can't determine any extremes from it and need to look at the rest of his head and body.

We can see worry lines over his eyes in both of these pictures, a sign that he can become concerned easily.

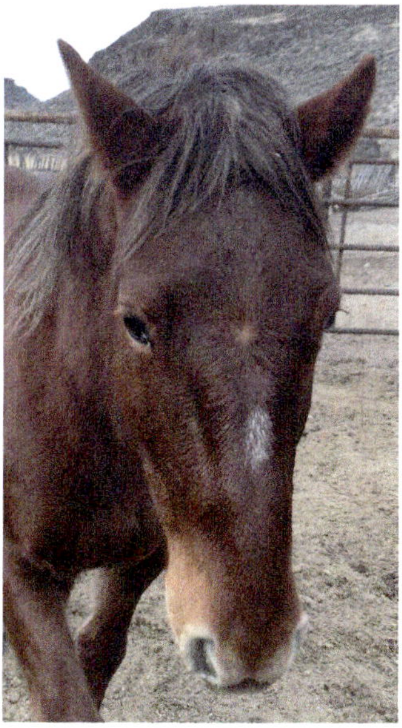

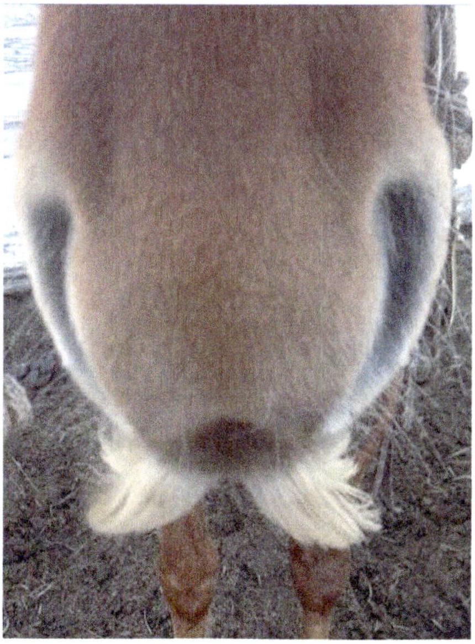

One of Mongrel's many charming features is his mustache. It grows longer and thicker in the winter. Mustaches are supposed to show quiet horses who will take care of their riders.

His ears are widely shaped and spaced, with more distance between the tips than the base. These are signs of a steady, willing horse. His upper lip is shapely and active. He will want to explore everything around him using it.

He has a single whorl to his left on the throatlatch. His one allowed rider says he tends to brace against the bit to the left.

All in all, he appears to be a very steady, dependable horse who is willing and tries hard to please his person.

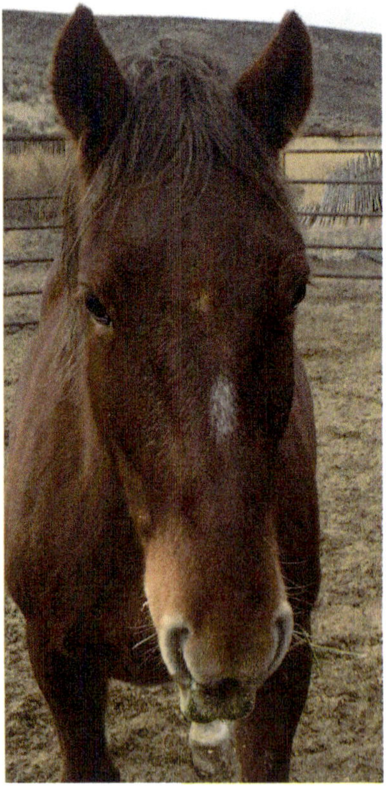

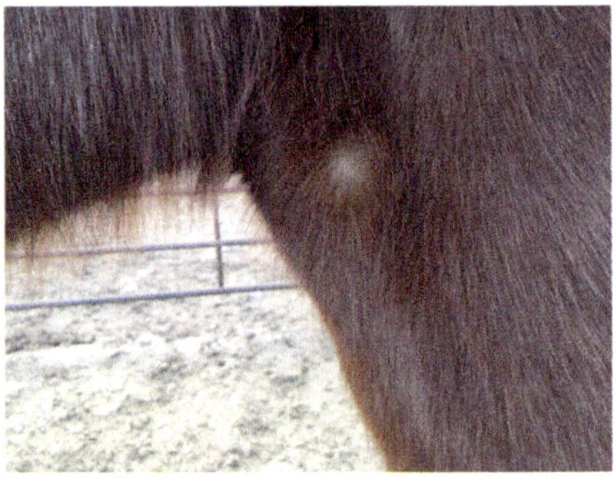

Mongrel's fear of people seems to come from nurture over nature, and it is emphasized by the tendency to worry. We can see this in the worry lines over his eyes. The stubbornness of his convex nose helps him to hang onto that worry instead of letting it go.

Princess Polliwog

Princess Polliwog, or Polly for short, is a BLM donkey adopted as a foal from the Bullfrog HMA in Nevada. When she came to Jen as a weanling, she was strongly bonded to an older donkey who had taken on a mothering roll for the young donkey. Luckily, Jen took them both.

Once home Jen had to watch out for Polly's hooves and teeth at all times. She hated being tied and would stomp, paw, and kick to show her displeasure.

Being strongly food motivated and extremely curious helped Polly to overcome her fear. Now she is a friendly in-your-space type of donkey, who is always inquisitive. Polly has been known to take entire hands into her mouth along with treats, but is learning better treat manners.

Just a yearling, Polly is being given time to grow and learn about life. Eventually, she will be started as a driving and riding donkey. Jen hopes to use her to represent mustangs and help educate people about them. She should have a lot to teach as she is a very unusual donkey.

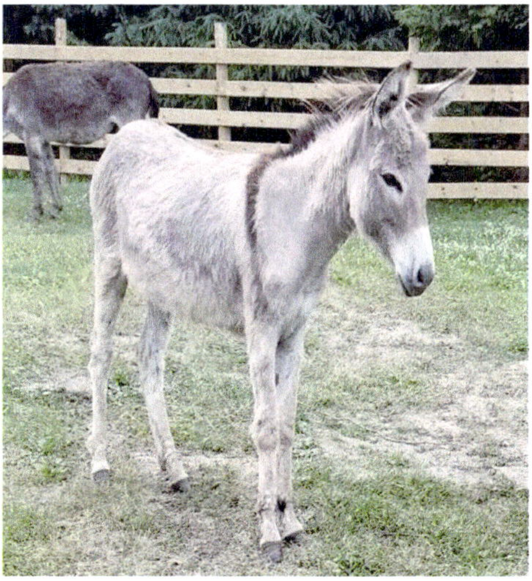

With a kind eye and a sweet face, Polly is a lovely young donkey.

Polly's whorl is very high for a donkey, nearly centered between her eyes.

In horses, whorls are set very near the location of the horse's olfactory lobes. A donkey's olfactory lobes are positioned differently than a horse's, they are are smaller and rotate inward. Donkey's whorls have been found to be located much farther away from the olfactory lobes and have no apparent relation to the position of the lobes.

That means we have to look at a donkey's whorls differently than we do a horse. This is the donkey equivalent of a high whorl!

Polly has a very straight, steady profile with a soft, easy going chin. Her ears prick sharply forward showing an energetic enthusiastic donkey.

Polly is a left-brain extrovert! This is unusual among donkeys who are typically thought to be introverts. Or are we letting those low whorls fool us when we should be judging donkeys by different standards than we do horses?

Miri

Sharon bought Miri from a horse trader. After getting her home, Sharon had her farrier out to remove Miri's shoes.

The farrier was horrified to see this horse. He told Sharon this was "THE" horse from over at that sleazy dealer's place. She had been there for months and was dangerous. When Sharon refused to immediately return the horse as he recommended, he told her, "lady, keep the horse. But you're going to go on the ride of your life".

Using the information on the Coggins test, Sharon found a history of Miri being sold and resold. One dealer in Kentucky told her, "if she was any good we would have sold her. There's a reason we sent her back to auction".

Sharon persisted despite the bad history and warnings that came with Miri. Using positive reinforcement, Sharon was able to get Miri to willingly accept a saddle and rider. At times she showed great promise, holding perfectly still when Sharon fell underneath her with one foot hung up in the stirrup. Miri watched calmly as Sharon pulled herself out from under her belly.

Other times she was triggered by her fears which would override all attempts to calm her. She would kick, bite, freeze, or panic.

Miri was never a happy horse. She hated other horses and people. She was making steps towards being able to be handled and, on her good days, would even stand loose to accept a saddle on her back then go at liberty to stand next to the mounting block.

One morning Miri was agitated when Sharon went to see her. She was lunging at animals over the fence from her and greeted Sharon at the gate with ears pinned back. Without further warning, Miri spun about and kicked Sharon, nearly killing her.

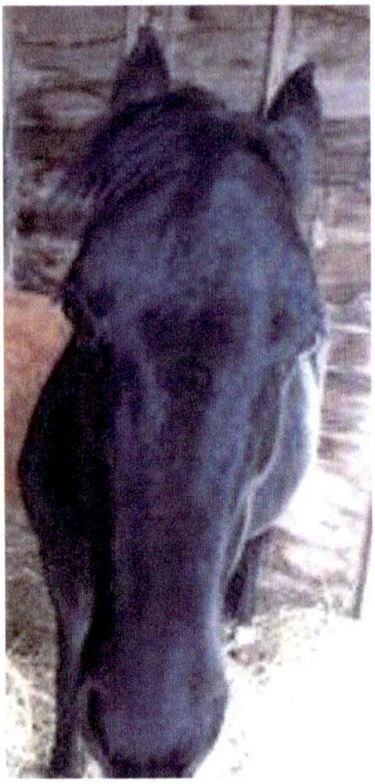

Miri's head is pretty basic, moderately wide between the eyes, she should learn easily.

She has a single center whorl. Nothing at all unusual there.

The ears are back in this photo. That is common when we are trying to get pictures of the head. It's much harder than one would think to get a good picture that shows what we need to see.

From the side, we can see a straight profile; no unusual bumps, no dish, nothing about her profile to suggest any difficulty.

Her jowl is moderately sized.

There is nothing about her head to show a horse who should have so much difficulty. Was it only her life experiences that caused her so much trouble?

Miri does have one unusual feature. In the center of her back, between the flanks, she has a whorl. A single whorl that is nearly impossible to see on a black horse. Sharon describes it as deep and tightly whorled.

A whorl is a focus point, we would expect to see something physical in relation to this whorl. Miri passed every vet exam with flying colors, never showing a hint of lameness.

Even without obvious outward signs of pain, is it possible that this whorl was causing her to feel unbalanced, maybe loose or uncoordinated though her hind quarters?

Was it her life of being passed from one horse trader to the next that caused her mental issues? Or did she get sent down that path when she was unable to handle how her body felt, causing her to act out?

We will never know for sure what caused Miri to be such a deeply troubled, unhappy horse. Nature and nurture together play strong roles in the eventual outcome of any horse. Perhaps, with the good careful training offered by Sharon, there would have been a time earlier in Miri's life when she could have been helped to be more comfortable in her body.

Unfortunately, by the time she finally reached a good home, she had experienced so much bad in life that there was no way to help her.

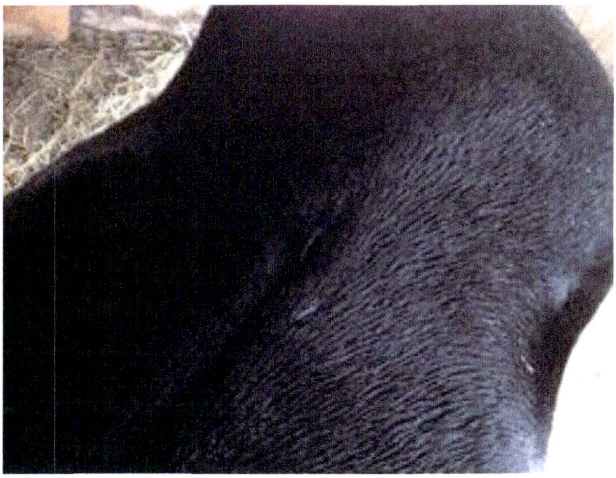

Tuck

Grace is a horse trainer who regularly takes mustangs to train for competition and as a TIP trainer. This time she was looking for a horse of her own. Tuck is a wild-born mustang from around Rock Creek, Nevada. Grace chose him out of the holding pens. The pens are chaotic, and the ability to look horses over carefully or to get an idea of their temperament ahead of time is limited.

So Grace concentrates on looking for overall conformation, soundness, and personality characteristics. Whorls are a great help in this sort of situation, if you are able to get close enough to see them. Tuck met all of the criteria and seemed to have a reasonably normal facial whorl.

At home, he was gentle and learned to halter and lead in a few short days. It soon became apparent that he had been shut down and was in a state of learned helplessness.

About a month into his training, he began to show a very reactive side. He panicked when standing tied, broke loose, and jumped through a large viewing window in the arena. Luckily Tuck wasn't hurt, but he will not stand tied now. When the lead rope is left lay he will stand all day.

Determined to please, he is anxious and anticipates every cue. After one day off of work, he needs a few days of work to get back in the groove. Once he gets going again he is an amazingly fast learner and picks up lessons after one try. Grace loves him, and despite his quirks, she will never let him go.

From the front we can see ears that are wide without a lot of curves, they have delicate points at the tips but that is the only definition showing that he should have some steadiness. The ears point straight up when pricked, showing an animated and energetic horse. His eyes are concerned but kind.

Eyes set far apart on a wide forehead that narrows down to a small muzzle show a quick learner. His upper lip is shapely and active; he will be a curious horse who wants to interact and explorer with his mouth.

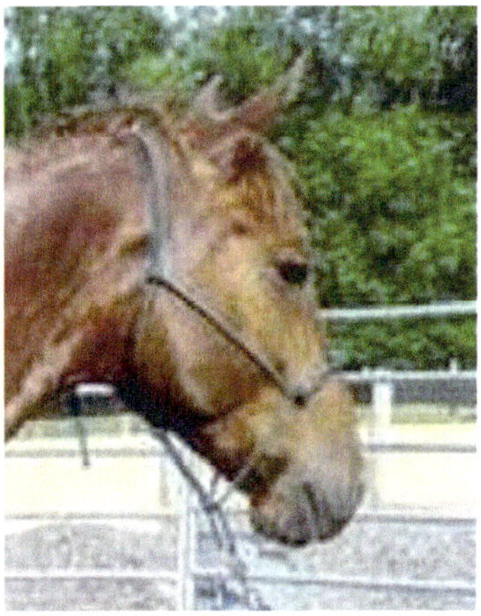

Although it is hard to see in these pictures, his whorl sits just above eye level and off slightly to our left. That shows a horse who should be brave, curious, and confident.

From the side, we see a mostly straight profile with a hint of a dish. His ears prick sharply forward. He shows a good bit of sensitivity and anxiousness.

Despite his desire to be confident and brave, he is overwhelmed by his nerves. An interesting combination of calm and scared, brave and timid, he shows a horse's ability to display more than one trait. Nothing is simple; personalities are complicated.

Hunter And Cloudy

Hunter is a Fjord stallion who rides and drives. His owner describes him as dependable, willing, cooperative, quiet, and a quick learner. He isn't bold, but he also isn't slow to approach novel objects. He's very logical and thinks things through before acting. If he gets hung up by a piece of harness or tack, he simply stands and waits patiently to be helped out of the situation. Hunter has passed down whorls in interesting and odd places to his foals, such as on the eyelids. However he has not yet thrown any replicas of his own whorls.

Cloudy is a young Quarter Horse gelding. He is used as a head horse for roping and to run barrels. Only recently started under saddle, he surprises everyone with his calm, willing demeanor. When something catches his attention, he doesn't spook, but heads over to investigate. He is described as lazy and gentle, a big pet, who is very personable.

Hunter and Cloudy, busy being good at their jobs

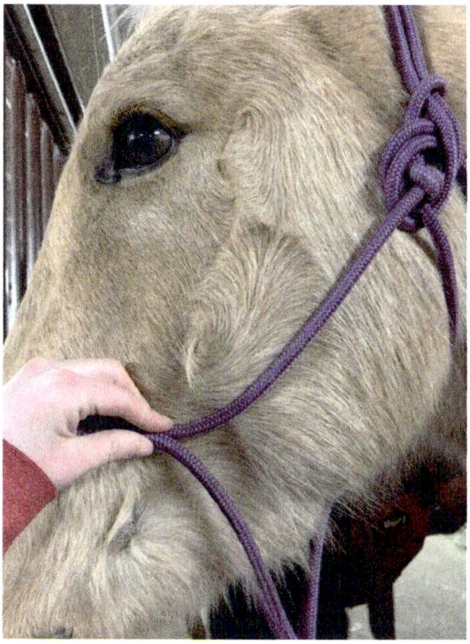

Cloudy and Hunter come from different breeds with completely different backgrounds, but they do have one characteristic in common. Both have three whorls down each side of their heads, one at the temple, one on the jowl, and one on the side of the jaw.

The whorl by the temple is supposed to signify a thinker, capable of coming up with all sorts of interesting ideas on their own.

The jaw and jowl whorls show a left-brain extrovert and can cause a horse to carry their jaws tight causing tension at the TMJ and from there, through the whole body.

Neither of these horses are worried about anything. They don't carry any tension and have never exploded when the pressure gets to be too much.

Is this a whorl pattern all its own instead of a combination of the separate whorls?

Smoke And Rusty

By a strange coincidence, both of these horses nearly became dog food because of a tendency to run people over.

Saved from near death, both became the trusted, preferred mounts of people who were willing to work with them instead of trying to make them listen by dominating them. A large part of the problem for both of these horses can be found in their whorls.

Smoke was a bottle-raised orphan who lived up to every possible bad stereotype we could expect from that. He was treated like a puppy and never learned how to 'speak horse'.

Once he was no longer cute and fun, he was dumped and then dumped again until a lady took him in out of pity and began to teach him how to function. He never did learn how to interact with other horses in the pasture. He missed small warnings and received large reprimands because of it. He was always the terror of people at the barn who expected a horse to stop when you stood in front of him. He would walk over or through anyone.

She took the time to teach him how to respond to cues and understand the basics of ground work through cooperation instead of coercion. He could not be forced to do anything if he didn't feel like it. He became safe to handle on the ground, although he once picked up his favorite small child by her hood and held her dangling there. She was happy, the adults were not.
He was dependable for anyone to ride. Scared of nothing and incredibly smart, he had a great sense of humor and would often scare other horses as he played with objects along the trail.

Rusty wasn't an orphan, but he was raised with the same bad manners and lack of foresight concerning what he would be like as a full-grown horse instead of a cute baby.

As a no longer cute yearling, he was dumped to go through different owners and sale barns until he ended up with a kill buyer. A rescue found him and was looking for someone who would take a horse who came with the warning that he would run you over.

They did find someone who thought fixing bad manners would be no big deal, and she offered to take him.

Fixing his bad manners was a big deal, and no amount of punishment phased him. He would still walk over and through anyone.

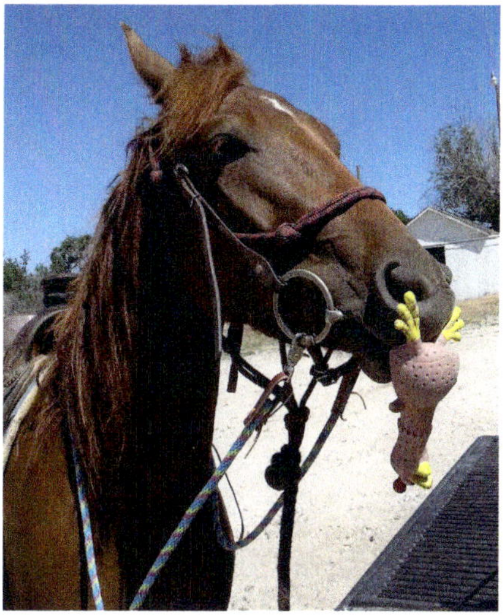

They don't look dangerous and aren't, not anymore.

Once they began to work together, and he was rewarded for good behavior instead of punishing the bad behavior, he decided he was willing to be a partner. As a partner, he became fearless and willing to do anything asked of him. Incredibly smart, it took only one lesson for him to grasp complicated ideas and invent new ones of his own. He could focus and work on a concept until he had it down.

As long as care was taken to keep him from getting confused, which upset him greatly, he was willing to do anything.

While the profiles show many differences, they are both convex, tough, and determined. They also share the same eyes, the look of eagles. These are proud individuals who are not easy but are great horses, overachievers, capable, and confident.

It may not look like it at first glance, but these two have the exact same whorl pattern. The black horse, Smoke, has a ghost whorl! Both of them have high double whorls with feathering coming up from the whorl farther to our left as we look at them. They both have straight to slightly convex profiles. That makes them left-brain extroverts, while the convex profile adds confidence and determination.

Both horses are bold, brave, and fearless. They would conquer the world if given the chance, there is no forcing these horses into compliance. If they recognize you as an equal and can be convinced that you are worth listening to they will do anything for you.

For a beginner or timid rider, these horses will be intimidating. For someone who wants to train with force, these horses will be a formidable opponent to break themselves on. For someone who appreciates intelligence and strength of character in a horse, they can be the horse of a lifetime.

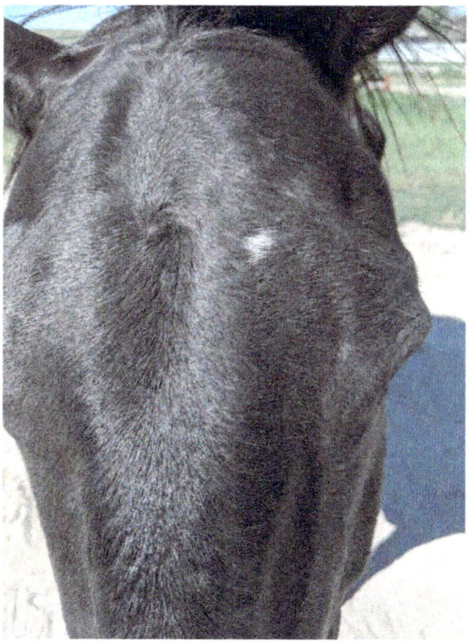

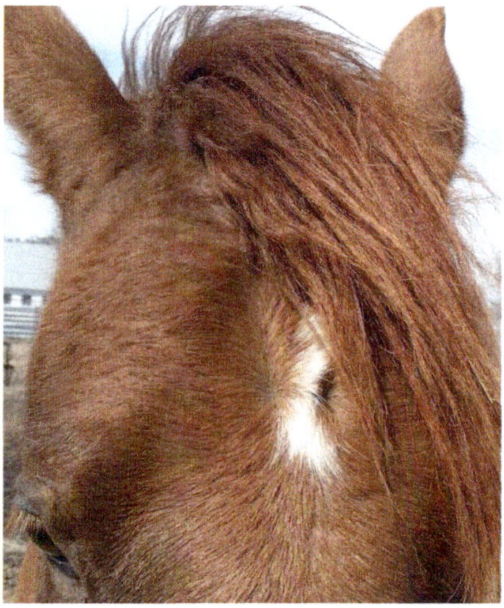

Harriet, Jerry, And Lady

These three horses share a very distinct head type. It is extremely refined, with skin tightly fit on a delicately sculpted head. They are sensitive and reactive while being completely sane and reliable, very solid citizens.

Jerry has won cow horse competitions, using all that sensitivity to get down and cut a cow. She is honest and completely the same in the arena as out. She is now a working ranch horse.

Lady has been an endurance and trail horse, but she is now a child's horse. She is extremely sensitive with lots of go, and completely quiet and trustworthy all at the same time.

Harriet is a non-ridden horse. She is well-loved by her person, and they both enjoy exploring the possibilities available to keep life as natural as possible in the domesticated world our horses live in.

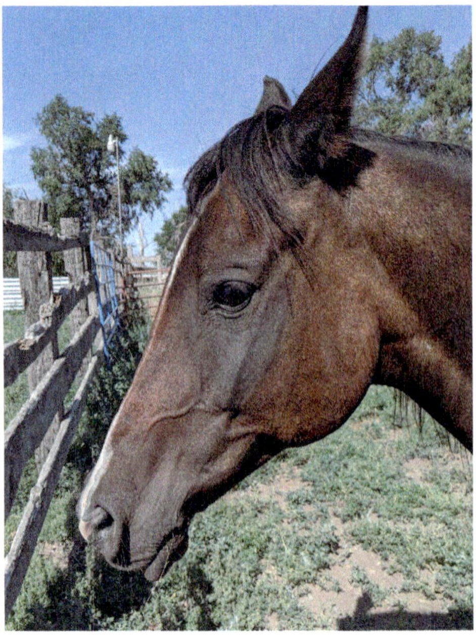

The chin is showing well here on Lady, even in her relaxed position. We can see the refined head, tightly fit skin, and wrinkles around the eye. She always seems tense, even when relaxed.

Along with having expressive skin that tends to wrinkle around the eyes and mouth more than normal, they also share a most unusual chin. These combine to allow them to show emotion strongly.

Almost normal looking when relaxed, the chin hardens and tightens to a sharp point when they are upset. The tightening pushes their lower lip forward to a rather comical extreme, extending far past the upper lip like a dinner plate. When the chin does this you can be guaranteed the skin will be wrinkled around the eyes to the point that the lids are pulled down, showing the pink around the inner eye.

Until the chin softens and relaxes, there is no point in trying to do anything with them. No training will be accomplished. They *may* be polite enough not to buck, but they will not be happy.

The chin can be helped to relax with massage, rubbing it until it softens. It can also be avoided by not putting them into stressful situations and being clear in your training.

That extremely fine, sensitive skin isn't only in looks. These horses tend to be bothered by bugs more than other horses, suffering from hives and terrible itching during bug seasons.

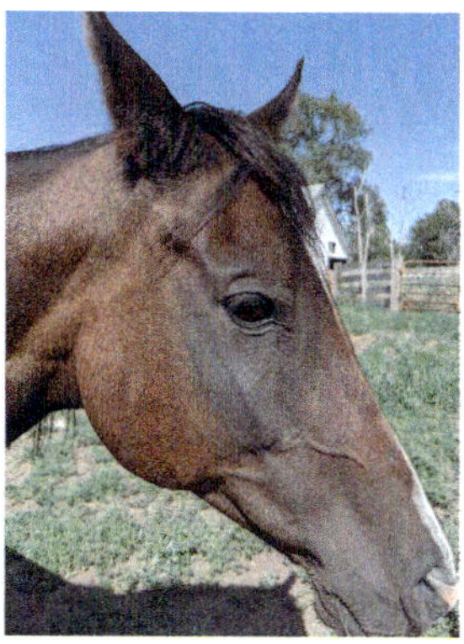

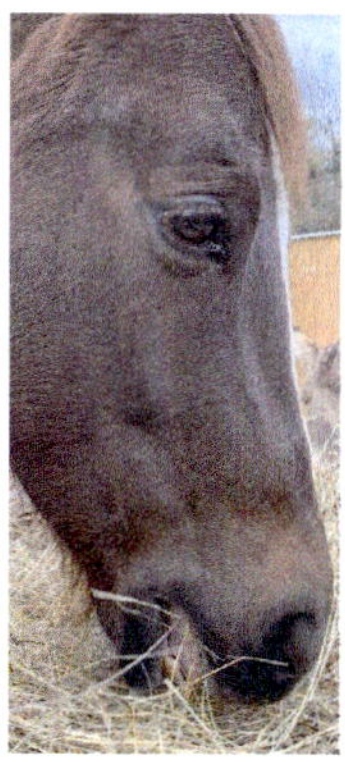

They share a mostly straight profile with a slight dish on a very rectangular head.

They have the same eyes, hard and round showing some nervousness. The lower lids often drawn down, exposing pink skin within.

Their ears are a bit on the hot side, shapely, and prick towards each other sharply.

Then there's that chin, mostly flat when relaxed, sharply pointed when stressed.

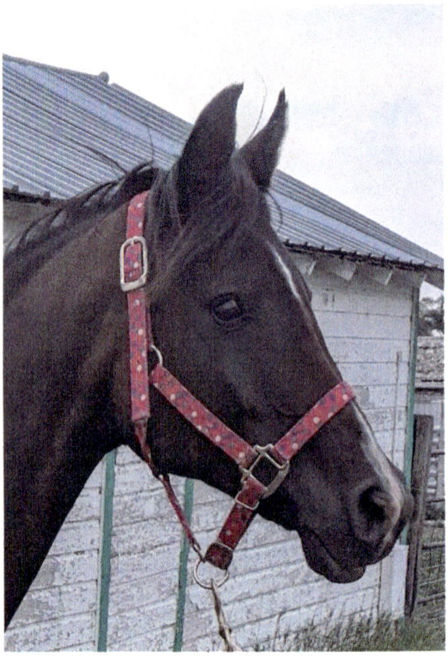

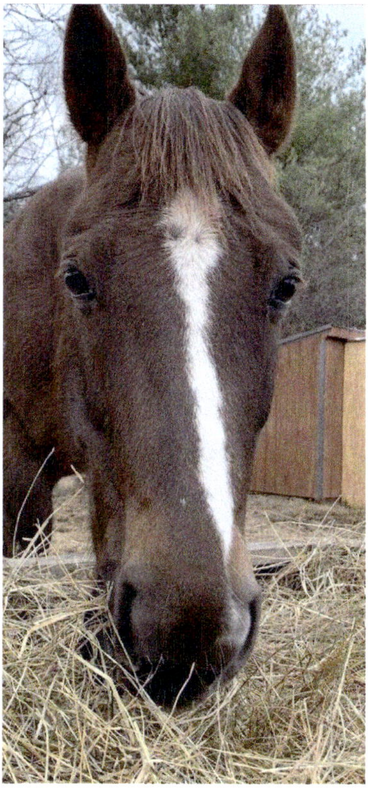

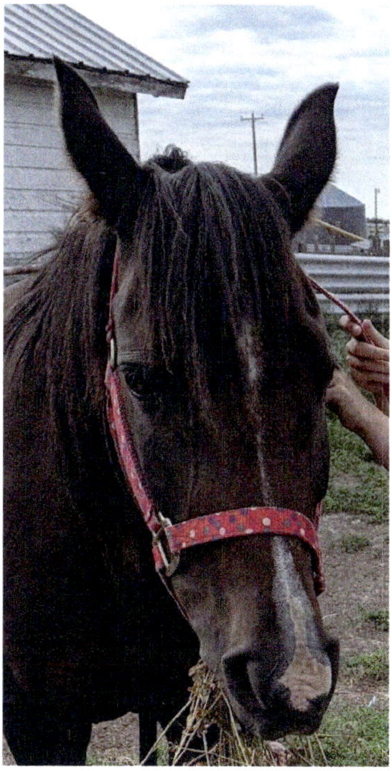

All three of these mares have long, narrow heads. They do best when lessons are explained clearly to avoid stress.

Their whorls are all very different, and they will have different temperaments to go with those whorls. The similarities in the shape of their chins, basic head shapes, and extra wrinkly skin tie them together. It is always exciting to see horses who have so much in common to compare.

About Noche

Noche grew up riding horses. That love of riding naturally turned to training as she grew older.

After graduating, Noche moved out west and spent some time working on ranches. She started taking in young horses to train. Having heard about whorl theory long ago, she paid attention to the whorls on horses who came in for training. The ones who were easy to start, as well as the tough ones.

She added her own notes to the backs of books about whorls and continued her studies.

No longer training horses for the public, she now concentrates on her small herd of problem horses. She is still focussing on whorls and how they affect the horses' movement and temperaments. The internet has allowed her to reach far more horses virtually than she was ever able to in person, and her studies aren't slowing at all.

For more horse whorl information and custom horse whorl analysis, join Noche at horsewhorls.com

Printed in Great Britain
by Amazon

81760636R00122